THE JEWS AMONG THE NATIONS

THE JEWS
AMONG THE NATIONS

ERICH KAHLER

With an Appendix

THE JEWS AND THE ARABS
IN PALESTINE

by Albert Einstein,
Erich Kahler, and Philip K. Hitti

FREDERICK UNGAR PUBLISHING CO.
NEW YORK

PREFACE

The three essays assembled in this volume form a coherent unit; they should be read in their present sequence,
like the successive chapters of a book. Their aim is to
show the character, the background, and the environmental situation of Jewish existence. The first essay, *What
Are the Jews?* is based on a lecture first given in 1950 and
somewhat elaborated since. The second essay, *The Jews in
Europe*, which gives an outline of Jewish history through
the ages, was written in 1945, but hitherto has not been
published. *The Jews and the Germans* is the partly revised
text of a lecture delivered at the Leo Baeck Institute in
New York in 1963.

This survey of the Jewish situation would have been
lacking without specific reference to the still persistent
controversy between the Jews and their immediate antagonists, the Arabs, over the justification of the State of
Israel. Therefore, to round out the picture, the text of a
dispute which Dr. Albert Einstein and I engaged in with
the Arab scholar, Dr. Philip K. Hitti, originally published
in 1944, has been included as an appendix.

E.K.

January 1967

Table of Contents

What Are the Jews?

ONE DAY when I was discussing the problem of anti-Semitism with the eminent Austro-Jewish poet, Richard Beer-Hofmann, he said to me: "I am not at all astonished at the fact that they hate us and persecute us. But what I cannot understand is, why they do not marvel at us more than they do."

Well, marveling at the strange phenomenon of the Jewish people would imply some knowledge of their history, some general perception of the Jewish destiny. And if there were such knowledge and such perception, there could not be so much hatred and persecution. But what seems to me more astonishing, and what I sometimes really worry about, is that the Jews themselves usually lack a sound knowledge of their history, that the Jews themselves do not marvel at the record of their history, at the sheer fact of their presence as Jews in our day, that they seem to have no true consciousness of the unique phenomenon they represent. I hold it to be a most urgent requirement in our critical times that the Jews be thoroughly aware of what they are and what they have stood for during thousands of years.

It must here be stated that what I mean by self-awareness is not to be identified with a certain parochial Jewish self-familiarity and self-indulgence, of which there is more than enough evidence. On the contrary, the self-awareness that I have in mind is to be sought as a necessary prerequisite for the understanding of a special responsibility which we bear before and for the world, and before and for the idea of our own historical existence. What are the Jews? To face this problem let us for a moment put ourselves in the position of the gentiles.

Among the non-hostile or even benevolent gentiles there is first the average *liberal* who will ask us: "What are you Jews and what do you want? If you truly want to be Americans, why can't you do away with your Jewish particularity? Why is it that you keep something apart from us, something which, moreover, implies a special and untrustworthy solidarity with your kindred in other countries?"

There are, to be sure, other ethnic stocks in this multi-national country, which represents a mirror, a replica of old Europe, indeed of the Old World, and not all of them have melted completely in the so-called melting-pot of American society. There are the Irish, the Italians, the Greeks, the Germans, and others, who all show a certain group adhesion, who cultivate their respective folk customs and traditions, and who also, in a larger or lesser degree, are concerned with the destinies of their people abroad. But there is a marked difference between the common reaction to the ethnic solidarity of these groups and that of the Jews. None of the other solidarities—with the temporary exception of the Japanese in the last war—has given rise to the question of divided loyalty, which has been made an issue in the case of Jewish support of the State of Israel. What we have to realize is the fact that the Jews have always been felt by the gentiles to be something more and something other than the representatives of a mere creed, and also as something apart from the unquestionably established nationalities.

A further step in this direction leads to the attitude of another group, the *extreme nationalists* who, for obvious reasons, have been less numerous and relevant in America than in more homogeneous countries of Europe. These people would tell us, in a not so friendly manner: "By your professing Judaism you actually admit that you belong to a different nationality, which within an indigenous nation can only claim the right of a tolerated minority, standing more or less outside the national community. It is not *our* fault that you have not succeeded in the course of time to preserve, or to build up, a national state large and strong enough to comprise and protect the whole of your people. With *us* you are mere guests, and you should abstain from interfering in our national affairs." This attitude borders on, and eventually leads to *racialism*, and the persecution cult of *Nazism*.

There is a third group, that of the *zealous Christian*, which keeps asking us the old question of two thousand years' standing: "Why do you, especially you Orthodox Jews, still cling to your fatal error of not acknowledging the gospel of Jesus Christ? Why do you insist upon your obsolete religion, which has become an arrogant heresy after its fulfillment by the Redeemer? All would be well if you all became Christians and gave up your old stubborn resistance."

And there is, finally, a fourth group, the *Socialists* and *Universalists* who tell us: "Why do you stick to *any* particularity at all? We are all men, human beings alike. Differences between people do not exist substantially, but are mere historical prejudices and results of economic disparities. You actually do the job of the Nazis by considering yourselves as a special group, as Jews. Why don't you merge with common humanity and cease altogether from being Jews *and* Americans or any other particular nationals?"

All these appeals reflect as many viewpoints of the gentiles as angles of the Jewish problem. In fact, many Jews react to these questions in one of the ways suggested to them by the gentiles. They not only comply with these suggestions, but are themselves convinced of the correctness and exclusiveness of the alternatives put before them.

We have among us *assimilates* who try to hide, to skip over their Judaism, to forget and make others forget that they are Jews; who want to be Americans and nothing else. Either they have become Christian converts, or they contend that Judaism is a mere creed and does not involve any kind of consanguinity, any relationship beyond a profession of faith that may be adopted or rejected at will.

We have, on the opposite side, the *Orthodox Jews*, who follow their old ritual way of life, expecting all solutions from God alone and shutting ears and eyes from what is going on around them, in passive and literal obedience to the religious commands.

We have, too, our *nationalists*, the *Zionists*, who hold that the Jews are just a nation like other nations, and that all we have to do is to support and strengthen the State of Israel.

And we have, finally, our *Socialists, Internationalists, Universalists* who, thoroughly indifferent to breed *and* creed, drive the assertion that "all men are born equal" (which is certainly valid inasmuch as human rights are concerned) to the extent of in effect denying the essential diversity of individual or ethnic dispositions.

So the attitudes of gentiles and Jews alike raise the puzzling question: *What are the Jews?* Are they a race, a nation, a creed, or nothing at all, just a result of certain accidental historical circumstances? Here we have, in fact, the first Jewish peculiarity: there is no other people in the world that would permit such a variety of interpretations.

It is easy to dispose of the first of these alternatives: the Jews are not a race, if we understand by this term a characteristic in the nature of a pure breed. The ultimate origins of peoples will forever remain indistinct, and all of them—the Jews are no exception—have in the course of history, to a higher or lesser degree, mingled with other ethnic stocks. So we may safely dismiss the assumption that the Jews are a race. But now the difficulties begin.

Let us consider next the contention that the Jews are in no way different from other human beings, and that whatever may appear to be particular Jewish traits are due solely to environmental, social, or economic conditions, and to tradition and education. This interpretation is no answer; it just pushes the question a little further back. I do not want to go into the complex problems of heredity and environment and of the inheritance of acquired characteristics. But the question remains: What are these conditions and traditions that produced the Jewish traits? What are they, and how did they arise?

It is true that the history of a people shapes its character. One could even go further and say: the history of a people *is* its character, the dynamic exposition of its character. But how much in this process is due to the within and how much to the without, how much to the internal configuration of initial stocks, and how much to the ever-changing external constellation of historical circumstances can hardly be determined, because a historical process is a mutual give-and-take between experience and reaction, it is a self-perpetuating interplay of "challenge and response," to use Toynbee's terms. So we do not gain anything by simply shifting the elements of Jewish particularity to circumstances and traditions. Circumstances are partly created and shaped by the individual or group that seems just to encounter them, and, conversely, traditions partly form as an answer to specific outer stimulations and demands. Circumstances and traditions of Jewish history belong to the character of the Jewish people; we could almost say they constitute the Jewish character.

So wherever we may place its origins, there exists a distinct Jewish character. That implies that we are not just plain human beings without any specific group characteristics, but that there exists a quality that distinguishes us as a group, that in some way sets us apart from other groups. This is demonstrated by evidence. First of all, by our own most immediate experience, by an indisputable feeling of kinship with fellow Jews. Such a feeling of kinship has nothing to do with personal relations, which may be much closer with gentile friends, nor has it to do with particular sympathy. It may even manifest itself inversely by a vehement irritation at Jewish peculiarities, by that well-known phenomenon of Jewish self-hatred, of which Karl Marx and Otto Weininger are conspicuous examples— something again that to such an extreme can hardly be found among other peoples. Theodor Lessing has written a very revealing study on this subject.

Let me quote a striking example of this feeling of kinship. Richard Beer-Hofmann, while in Berlin for the rehearsals of one of his plays, was coming up the stairs of the Berlin subway; it was a cold, windy winter night, and his face was wrapped in a woollen scarf so that only his eyes could be seen. An old Orthodox Jew in his caftan came down the stairs and stopped him. "The gentleman is one of us [*Der Herr ist einer von uns*]," he said to Beer-Hofmann, "he will tell me how I can get to the Nollendorfplatz." The eyes alone were enough to reveal a Jew to a Jew.

The distinct Jewish particularity is evidenced by innumerable stories, sadly funny stories, self-deriding stories, which, all of them, deal with the peculiar conditions, experiences, and attitudes of Jewish people, not simply those who believe in Judaism.

So it seems as if our Zionists were right in assuming that we are a nation, just like the British, the French, the Italians, and that, accordingly, we must behave like a modern nation. But there is something that very strikingly distinguishes us from those modern nations, and this is the fact that we have a religion of our own, and that this religion played a decisive role in shaping the destiny and the very character of the Jewish people, much more intrinsically than did Christianity in influencing the development of Western nations. Not only is this religion uniquely our own, for we do not share it with any other group of people— with the one exception of the remnants of the Khazars, who collectively adopted Judaism in the eighth or ninth century A.D., and whose remnants were extinguished by Hitler—but this religion forms part of all that is Jewish, even of the thoroughly secularized life of modern Jews. To be sure, other religions too have cast their stamp on secular manners, have brought about special modes of thought and approach in people's lives. So we may rightly speak of a Catholic or a Puritan mentality, even in people who have ceased to go to church, or to take part in religious gatherings. But when we compare the life of a truly Orthodox Jew, which in its minutest details is controlled by religious commands, taboos, and rituals, with the life of even the most ardent Catholic or Protestant who, apart from duly attending his church services, communions, and confessions, or his community prayers, singing, and contemplations, is left free to lead his daily life as he sees fit, we can notice the difference of the impact and the effects which Jewish and Christian religions have had on the disposition of their followers. It is true that Catholicism, and in a much stricter degree Puritanism have, through their precepts and attitudes, exerted an influence also on the secular life of their faithful. But even the sternest rulings of Puritanism, bordering on worldly asceticism, never penetrated so deeply into the physical disposition of the human being as did the Jewish rituals. Jewish existence is wholly imbued with the modes and manners of the Jewish religion. Such distinct personalities as Heine, who was a skeptic, an intellectual adventurer, as Spinoza, as Kafka, whose devotion was entirely unorthodox, unfixed, exploratory, as Bernard-Lazare, who was a freethinker, and as Werfel, who was almost a Catholic—all of them show attitudes and proclivities clearly deriving from the Jewish religion.

A particular zeal in pursuing ideological aims, in drawing practical consequences from ideological aims, an eager intensity and tenseness in all performances of life, which to gentiles is a somewhat baffling phenomenon—all this betrays a fundamentally religious attitude. Jewish dialectics and witticism, which often are misunderstood as extreme intellectualism, stem, in fact, from rather irrational sources: they trace back to a religious stance of generations, to the age-old dialogue with God. And were one to scrutinize the roots of many a Jew's mode of behavior, were one to psychoanalyze him, the multifold, minute peculiarities, the crazy, superstitious, neurotic habits that we sometimes observe in such persons would turn out to be the remnants of submerged ritual customs, of ritual "archetypes." Certain compulsion neuroses and dietary aversions are secularized, automatized residues of the ritual. Even that typically Jewish self-denial that sometimes grows into outright self-persecution betrays a subconscious, indeed physical bad conscience, a furious striving to get rid of a bond that cannot by any means be totally eradicated.

From all this we may conclude that the Jews are an ethnic group, but one that differs from the national groups around it by having a religion of its own, and by being deeply rooted in its religion. This religion, in turn, differs from the Christian, Islamic, and Buddhist world religions in that it is exclusively connected with a special ethnic group, and that this connection is in the nature of the closest characterological, we may almost say biological, ties.

Hence there exists a very real Jewish "consanguinity," and yet this consanguinity is not a *purely* physical, not a mere "blood"-relationship, after the concept of modern racialists or geneticists. The characterological ties of the Jews were created by the Jewish religion in a stage of humanity when body and spirit, physical and psychic life, had not yet parted; when not only physical urges and conditions affected man's psyche, but psychic and spiritual experiences impressed themselves on the body with such an immediacy and penetrative force as can hardly be imagined by the intellectual and at the same time materialistically oriented sophisticates of our age. Thus, on a more primitive level, it was and is even possible for persons of alien extraction to become, through close communion with Jewish groups, so thoroughly Judaized that they assume even physical Jewish traits.

The Jews distinguish themselves from a nation as clearly as Judaism differs from a creed; that is, from a mere profession of faith. Considering these features of the Jewish phenomenon we may say that the Jews are originally, and essentially, a *tribe*.

For a full understanding of what is meant by the above statement, it is necessary briefly to clarify the significance of certain terms that I have used: *nation, tribe, religion, creed*. I believe that one should not use terms loosely, especially in the present turmoil of political, colloquial, and scholarly talk. I do not care about words in themselves, for they may be substituted by other words. But I do care about the exact meaning of the distinctive phenomena for which they stand. There is a precise difference between a religion in its true sense, and a creed or dogma, or profession of faith. And there is a corresponding difference between a tribe and a nation.

Religion in its original sense is not the same thing as adherence to the purely spiritual dogma of a *world religion*. True religion is not something one can adopt or drop at will, by a plain act of conviction. It is a deep, inalienable bond, permeating the whole of a man's existence, and compelling him to treat every happening, every experience, every reaction and gesture of his life, even physical life, in relation to a metaphysical being or concern.

Hence genuine, original religion is more than a purely individual attitude. It is at the same time a specific, pri-

meval form of human community: a community beyond all
visible organization, a community that does not need organization of any kind, since it is held together by a common
attachment to a sublime, supreme being that expresses the
essence, the life-giving principle of the community—all that
its people cherish, adore, love, and aim at, in life.

An ethnic group, a social structure that is founded on
such metaphysical, more than physical, substance and communion, a group that has grown out of religion, and whose
primal core is religion, such a group may be called a *tribe*.
It is fundamentally different from a *nation*, which is a
wholly secular folk organism, and whose life is centered in
a completely worldly form of ethnic culture and development. To the nation, religion has come from without, as a
universal religion, pre-established in a separate sphere, un-
connected with the ethnic structure of a people. A world
religion does not appeal to any group, it appeals solely and
immediately to the individual. It has become a dogma, a
creed—that means a credo—which any individual, regardless of ethnic origin, may profess.

To sum up, a *tribe* is an ethnic group that has evolved
out of and with its proper religion and *before* the development of a world religion, or out of its reach. A *nation* is
an ethnic group that came into being *after* the development
and under the aegis of a world religion, as did France,
England, Russia, and other countries. The substratum of
a nation has nothing to do with religion, however strong
the influence of a world religion on its development. The
essentially mundane elements interacting toward the forma-
tion of this substratum are: language, the nature of the
country, the physiognomical, characterological and be-
havioral types of the people, and that secular heir and sub-
stitute of original religion, *tradition*—that is, the residual
manifestation of a social and intellectual civilization.

So the Jews appear to be, by origin and authentic nature,

a *tribe*, a primordial social structure, and hence, in spite of their dispersion the closest related of historical communities, closer related among each other than the locally associated members of a modern nation. In the Orthodox Jews we have still with us the prototype of that primordial core of Israel.

But searching deeper into the Jewish phenomenon, we come upon a paradox that constitutes the actual uniqueness of this ethnic community: no other particular people has been so constantly and immediately involved and concerned in the destiny of humanity at large; no other people's individuality was so intrinsically interwoven with genuine *universality*. From its early beginnings Jewish religion, the foundation and essence of the Jewish tribe, had a universal scope; from the outset its teachings and the career of its tiny people aimed at mankind. Thus the Jewish character combines narrowest particularity with true universality. Indeed *the substance of its particularity is universality*.

This combination made for an existence that was fraught with peril. Both these extremes, separately and jointly, alternately and concurrently, acted as a constant challenge to the peoples of the world; they were the source of that persistent hostility of the other peoples toward the Jews. And yet it is this very combination that helped the Jewish people to survive; to survive their earthly, political organization, to survive unparalleled persecutions and sufferings, to survive in so many forms and disguises. Their particularity supported their universality, and vice versa; and this mutual support carried Judaism along through history.

Let us briefly glance at this unique career of a people. It is, first of all, universal in *time*. The Jews are one of the most ancient historical peoples living today; they are about 3200 years old and are still very much alive. The Chinese go back historically to about 1700 B.C., the Indian Aryans to about the end of the second millennium B.C. But the Chinese as well as the Indians stayed on in their vast homelands where they developed into enormous, physically inextinguishable populations. The Jews have always been numerically a small people; they have never exceeded the fifteen million which was their number before the Hitler massacre. The Chinese, as well as the Indians, though achieving very high and refined cultures, have, in their comparatively remote areas, been arrested in a certain stage of human evolution; only very recently and forcibly are they catching up with the blessings and curses of modern civilization. On the other hand the Jews, in their cultural and intellectual development, have paralleled human evolution through all its phases; their history circumscribes the evolution of humanity. Indeed Jewish history is a special version of world history. A prominent Jewish historian, Simon Dubnov, rightly called his standard work *World History of the Jewish People.*

But this history of a particular people is equally universal in *space*, earthly as well as spiritual space. Although crystallizing around a tiny homeland, Jewish life spread over most of the globe, and into all domains of intellectual activity.

From the first, we notice in Jewish history a strange detachment from the locale. Jewish history is the only history we know of that started in exile, from a homeless, alien, and oppressed condition. There are many peoples whose career began with migrations and invasions; there is none, however, which actually began with an exodus and a wandering toward an imaginary land, as was the experience of the Jewish people.

Even the Founding Father, Abraham, who incidentally was believed to be the originator of a much wider web of kinship than Israel, left Ur in search of a home. And the pilgrimage of Israel from Egypt to a blessed land, carried out under the leadership of a unifying God, whose concept was formed during the wandering, and who therefore became a nomad God, not confined to any special place, nor to be conjured up in any image or name, this pilgrimage, still a plainly physical one, is a prefiguration of the world-wide pilgrimage of the people of Israel through human history, which was to come later. As Charles Péguy, a gentile who knew more about the Jews than many Jews themselves, put it: "The most comfortable houses, the best built from stones . . . the most real of real estate . . . will never mean any more to [the Jews] than a tent in the desert. . . . And for us [the gentiles], on the contrary, the canvas of tents was already, will always be, the stone of our houses."

Thus, from the very beginning, the trend and the end of Jewish history was established: first, by exile, wandering, and the dream of a holy land; and subsequently, consequently, by the special character of the Jewish God, the everlasting and omnipresent, the imageless and nameless, the one and only one, the creator and not created, without theogony and mythology, the zealous and jealous one, Who did not tolerate any other God beside Him, while for all purely tribal gods it was only claimed that they were mightier than, not exclusive of, others.

Hence, the Jewish God, with His claim to be the only one, with His invisibility and spirituality, was implicitly a universal God, Who was aiming at all human beings as images of Himself, and to Whom the children of Israel were *only* His "chosen people." I say *only*, meaning: to the Jewish God the children of Israel were not intrinsically identical with humanity proper, as were the Egyptians, the Babylonians, the Persians, to their deities. The Jews did not believe that they represented the whole of mankind; and they did not develop a concept of barbarism, such as had even been entertained by so advanced a people as the Greeks, to whom the alien was not until very late in history, not even potentially, a full member of the human community. Though it has been interpreted as an arrogant prerogative, the tenet of the "chosen people" is in fact a *limitation*. Looking backward, in the perspective of modern nations, it does of course seem like arrogance, but one has to consider it in the context of the general human condition of the epoch in which it arose.

The meaning of the idea of the chosen people can be properly understood only in its connection with another, much more fundamental Jewish concept, a concept that is unique in the whole ancient world, confirming as it does the universality of the Jewish God and at the same time establishing the freedom of man. I mean the concept, and the tenet, of the Covenant, which implies that not only has God chosen the Jewish people, but that the Jewish people, on their part, have chosen God. It also implies that God was originally taken to be the God of all peoples. This is further indicated by the story of the creation, and more explicitly still by the story of the Tower of Babel (Genesis 11), which makes it quite evident that God was originally the God of all men: "Behold, the people is one, and they have all one language." God's creation of the diversity of mankind confirms mankind's original unity.

The special relation between God and the people of Israel was instituted through a formal agreement. It was based on trust. The other peoples, so it was implied, ignored the call of God. Only Abraham "believed in the Lord," according to Genesis 15:6, and 22:18: "And in thy seed shall all the nations of the earth be blessed; because thou hast obeyed my voice." The Covenant has been confirmed by God to Isaac: "I will perform the oath which I swore unto Abraham, thy father" (Genesis 26:3), to Jacob (Exodus 2:24), and to the people of Israel through Moses (Exodus 6:4, 19:5; Deuteronomy 26:17-18): "Thou hast avouched the Lord this day to be thy God and to walk in His ways, and to keep His statutes, and His commandments, and His judgments. . . . And the Lord hath avouched thee this day to be His peculiar people, as He hath promised thee." The idea of the Covenant, as it is clearly expressed in this bilateral statement of relationship, which sounds like a treaty, is that man is represented as a free partner of God. For the first time, the relation between God and man has been put on a legal basis, and not only in regard to its treaty character, but also concerning the substance of the Covenant, which consists of a legal code to be observed by the people of Israel, the very condition for their being chosen as God's "peculiar people." This legal basis accounts for the crucial importance of the Law in Jewish religion. For the Law was claimed to be binding not only for man, but also for God. To what extremes deeply pious Jews were driven in maintaining their claim may be seen from the uncanny Hasidic story about a man's lawsuit against God, in which the plaintiff won.[1]

---

[1] "The Emperor in Vienna issued an edict which was bound to make thoroughly miserable the already oppressed Jews in Galicia. At that time, an earnest and studious man by the name of Feivel lived in Rabbi Elimelekh's House of Study. One night he rose, entered the zaddik's room, and said to him: 'Master, I have a suit against God.' And even as he spoke he was horrified at his own words.

"But Rabbi Elimelekh answered him: 'Very well, but the court is not in session by night.'

"The next day, two zaddikim came to Lizhensk, Israel of Koznitz and Jacob Yitzhak of Lublin, and stayed in Rabbi Elimelekh's house. After the midday meal, the rabbi had the man who had spoken to him called, and said: 'Now tell us about your lawsuit.' 'I have not the strength to do it now,' Feivel said falteringly.

" 'Then I give you the strength,' said Rabbi Elimelekh.

"And Feivel began to speak. 'Why are we held in bondage in this Empire? Does not God say in the Torah: "For unto Me the children of Israel are servants." And even though He has sent us to alien lands, still wherever we are, He must leave us full freedom to serve Him.'

"To this Rabbi Elimelekh replied: 'We know God's reply, for it also is written in the passage of reproof through Moses and the prophets. But now, both the plaintiff and the defendant shall leave the courtroom, as the rule prescribes, so that the judges may not be influenced by them. So go out, Rabbi Feivel. You, Lord of the world, we cannot send out, because Your glory fills the earth, and without Your presence not one of us could live for even a moment. But we herewith inform You that we shall not let ourselves be influenced by You either.'

But what is the real meaning of the "peculiarity," the "chosenness" of the Jewish people? What is meant by the affirmation "In thy seed shall all the nations of the earth be blessed"? It does not mean just a privilege, but a mission, indeed the *privilege of a mission,* for the one does not exist without the other. The Jews were God's chosen people only with regard to a special task which He would entrust to them. They were to become God's experimental case of excellence, God's model for humankind, the "light to the Gentiles," as it was later proclaimed by Isaiah (chap. 49). Even in Exodus 19:6 this is pronounced in the words of God: "And ye shall be unto me a kingdom of priests, and a holy nation." It is repeated in Deuteronomy 26:19 in connection with the demand "to keep God's statutes and His commandments. . . ."

The demand in its rigidity was, of course, too much for the Jewish people to fulfill, and the Jews had to suffer the extreme castigation, which was the reverse of their missionary election, and which was threatened in the terrifying prophesy of Deuteronomy 28:

> "And the Lord shall scatter thee among all people, from the one end of the earth even unto the other. . . . And among these nations shalt thou find no ease, neither shall the sole of thy foot have rest: But the Lord shall give thee there a trembling heart, and failing of eyes, and sorrow of mind. And thy life shall hang in doubt before thee; and thou shalt fear day and night and shalt have none assurance of thy life. . . . And thou shalt become an astonishment, a proverb, and a byword, among all the nations whither the Lord shall lead thee . . . and thou shalt be only oppressed

"Then the three sat in judgment silently and with closed eyes. After an hour, they called Feivel and gave him the verdict: that he was in the right. In the same hour, the edict in Vienna was cancelled." (Martin Buber, *Tales of the Hasidim,* Vol. I, *The Early Masters* [New York, 1947], 258-59)

and crushed alway: so that thou shalt be mad for the sight of thine eyes, which thou shalt see." [2]

The trend and the end of Jewish history was instituted from the beginning, last but not least by the special character of the Divine commands, which connected a tribal ritual, governing every move of human life, with the first truly moral code in history; that means, with precepts concerning man's behavior toward his fellow men, not fellow kinsmen. It was not only the first law on earth to ordain "love thy neighbor as thyself" (Leviticus 19:18), but it was the very first to show a special regard for the alien, to set down a command like this: "The stranger that dwelleth with you shall be unto you as one born among you, and thou shalt love him as thyself; for ye were strangers in the land of Egypt." [3]

These commands have been considered to be the essence of Judaism by the great spiritual leaders of the Jewish people. There is a story about Hillel: A gentile was said to have called on him and pledged that he would embrace Judaism if Hillel were able to tell him all the teachings of the Torah while he himself could bear standing on one foot. "Love thy neighbor as thyself," was Hillel's immediate answer, "all the rest is just explanation and illustration." Thereupon the stranger converted to Judaism. Akiba also called this command the fundamental principle of the code. And this command with all its broad implications meant, in the last analysis, the establishment of true brotherhood among human beings, of a realm of peace, of united humanity. This Israel was to propagate among the gentiles, this was to be the basic content of its mission.

[2] Deuteronomy 28:64 ff.; 37:33 ff.
[3] Leviticus 19:34. This command is one of the oldest. It is similarly expressed in the twenty-third chapter of Exodus, belonging to the so-called Book of the Covenant, which dates from the ninth century B.C., and the contents of which, judged by the archaisms, trace back to an even earlier period.

So we see that Judaism from its very beginning has represented a connection between two seemingly contradictory elements. The substance, the foundation, the life principle of a particular human community, the Jewish tribe, is at the same time a principle to be valid for humanity as a whole. The Everlasting is the tribal God of the Jews, who are His preferred, His chosen people, and with whom He has concluded a special Covenant, and, on the other hand, He claims to be, and is claimed to be, a universal God, the God of all the peoples of the world. And it is the same with His commands, which tie down in a most uncompromising way the highest and purest aims of humanity to a primeval, strictly tribal ritual, governing every practical and physical act of the individual.

In this apparently paradoxical connection is held the essence of the Jewish character and the Jewish people, which we may call a tribe directed toward the achievement of an all-embracing, supra-ethnic humanity.

The paradox finds its resolution when we understand it as an evolutionary process, as the long, dramatic process of Jewish history and the continuous dialectic struggle within each successive generation, within all the groups and individuals of which the Jewish people have been composed.

After the Jews had settled down in Palestine around 1200 B.C. (that is to say, those Jews who had set out from Egypt under the leadership of Moses, and among whom the revolutionary concept of the Everlasting had taken definite shape) they developed states and temporarily a united state, just like the other peoples around them. And in this period the tribal particularity prevailed. The Everlasting was a tribal God among other tribal gods, and the stern, indeed violent maintenance of His commands, even of His moral commands and of His attributes of spirituality and universality, was chiefly meant to preserve just the physical body, the particularity and purity of Israel.

Yet, the Jewish states were small and futile, though they had splendid moments and were valiantly defended. The Jews, numerically a little people, could never have upheld their tiny homeland against the mighty kingdoms that overran it, even if their religion had not from the outset had so spiritual a basis, so inimical to the power of the state. The political failure appears actually to have been conceived as an integral part of Jewish destiny. In Deuteronomy 7:7-8 it is said: "The Lord did not set His love upon you nor choose you because ye were more in number than any people; for ye were the fewest of all people: but because the Lord loved you." And in Hosea 17, God says: "I will have mercy upon the house of Judah and will save them . . . and will not save them by bow, nor by sword, nor by battle."

However, by virtue of that spiritual nature of their tribal religion, the Jews, for all their weakness, outlasted the powers by which they were subdued. The ominous date of 586 B.C., the time of the conquest of Jerusalem by the Babylonians, was in fact the historical birth date of true Judaism. That spiritual community of the Jews that later spread all over the world was founded upon the loss of their earthly community.

In the Palestinian homeland the purified monotheistic concept of an imageless creator of the world had been grasped only by an elite. Now, in the exile, the uprooted masses were pervaded by it. The *priesthood* assumed a new character: having been a caste with a ritual function, it now became a spiritual profession. The priests became scribes, they elaborated the priestly code and prepared the Torah as the constitution of Judaism.

The other, the unofficial line of religious tradition, that of the *prophets*, reached its high point in Ezekiel and

Deutero-Isaiah. The prophets freed religion from the official forms of worship, they drove it deeper into the mind of individual man, and stirred in him a sense of personal responsibility. They were the first to bring into the foreground the universal and missionary quality of this religion, which led to the Essenes and to Christianity.

In these times, in fact, not only was Judaism established in its consummate form, but implicity there came into being all elements of what may be considered *true Christianism*: universality, spirituality, human brotherhood, mission, and also the reverse of this mission—humility and martyrdom. In Isaiah 53:3-6 the heathen were to say of Israel: "He is despised and rejected of men; a man of sorrows and acquainted with grief: and we hid, as it were, our faces from him. He was despised, and we esteemed him not. Surely he hath borne our griefs, and carried our sorrows; yet we did esteem him stricken, smitten of God, and afflicted. But he was wounded for our transgressions, he was bruised for our iniquities: the chastisement of our peace was upon him; and with his stripes we are healed." And Israel speaks of himself (Isaiah 50:6): "I gave my back to the smiters, and my cheeks to them that plucked off the hair; I hid not my face from shame and spitting." These are not Christian words, these are genuine Jewish words uttered centuries before Jesus was born. They were only used by the Christian tradition as an anticipation of Jesus' deed and teachings.

In the succeeding Persian period again a tightening and particularizing of the Jewish community took place in the reform of Ezrah, which was intended to preserve and fortify the body of Israel. And in the subsequent Hellenistic period, after the conquests of Alexander, the two tendencies, the particularistic, ritualistic, bodily tribal, and the spiritual and universal, were active side by side and were developing into a furious antagonism. Gradually they permeated each other, they grew together and began to form that tragically dialectic character that has marked Judaism and the Jewish people ever since.

Both tendencies were indispensable, though. For the Jews, dispersed as they were over the entire globe, were enabled to maintain themselves only by the indissoluble union of the sternly spiritual and universal religious idea with a strictly exacting tribal ritual. The ritual was the means to the physical survival of the people, because an abstract law, particularly one of such ethical severity, could not possibly hold the masses together. Some physical prompting was needed, some magic signposts had to be kept to guide the people through the earthly misery and alienation of their life in the Galuth. Yet, the ritual alone, without its dignification by a spiritual and universal law, would have become meaningless and obsolete. It would have perished like so many pagan cults.

The combination of extreme particularity with extreme universality was implicitly the source of that special hostility that the Jews encountered in various forms throughout their history. It appeared for the first time also in the Hellenistic period; the Greeks and the Romans inaugurated it. From the outset, the primary cause of anti-Judaism has been the linking of the two intransigences: the ritual and the spiritual.

The Greeks and the Romans were well acquainted with magic cults and rituals; they had full understanding of this mode of life. And on the other hand, in Neo-Platonic and Stoic philosophy they had reached a spiritual conception of humanity. But what caused them apprehension and irritation was the twofold character of Judaism, its existence on two levels at the same time.

Characteristically, the Jews were for the first Greek observers "a tribe of philosophers" [4] or "the philosophers' caste

---

[4] Theophrastus, *On Piety.*

of the Syrians," [5] to be compared with the Indian Brahmins.
If Judaism was a philosophy, they wondered, why did it
not allow that individual liberty of thinking and of living
the Greeks were accustomed to find in their own philosophers? Why did the Jews tie a highly spiritual doctrine to
a tribal ritual, to circumcision, that was identified with cas-
tration, to dietary laws, formulas of prayer, Sabbath rest,
and a disciplined piety of utmost strictness? But if there
were worship and ritual, why were there no images, no
names for God? Why no palpable deity, who could have
intercourse with the gods of other cults, who could be compared or even linked with them? Why, among men too, that
ritual exclusiveness of the Jewish communities in the all-
amalgamating crowd of Hellenistic people? Why the refusal to take part in the meals, in the games, in the whole
gay life of the pagans? The people attracted by the ethical
teachings were not inclined to take the ritual along with
the rest. The masses, on the other hand, at home on the
cultic level, were repelled by the rigor of the cult, and regarded it as an arrogance.

The Hellenistic civilization with its social intermixture
and intellectual activity was a dangerous temptation for the
Jews. It was their first contact with a civilization that was
on a spiritual par with Judaism, but at the same time more
graceful, colorful, sensuous, gregarious, and therefore
likely to lure them into surrender.

To counter this temptation both tendencies in Judaism
were again at work: the tribal, ritual-minded priestly orthodoxy and the spiritual, universal trend, set forth by the last
of the great prophets, Jesus of Nazareth.

The conflict that arose between these two forces has been
obscured by the later Christian interpretation. To be sure,
it concerned the validity of the Jewish Law. But it had
nothing to do either with the content or with the spirit of
the Law. It had nothing to do with the precepts for man's

[5] Klearchus of Soloi in Josephus: *Contra Apion.*

behavior toward his fellow men. On these principles both factions agreed completely.[6]

What this struggle was actually about was the maintenance of the ancient constitution of Israel; that is, the integral theocracy of Israel, God being represented by the impersonal Law as originally instituted by Him. The issue was, whether man, whether a person, be he ever so inspired, should decide on what is right or wrong, or whether this decision should rest with the impersonal Divine Law. Consequently, whether a person should be permitted to determine what part of the Law is essential—that is, in accord with its spirit—and what, on the other hand, was merely dictated by temporal, materially expedient, and possibly transient exigencies.

Jesus gave the strongest expression to the old prophetic tendency: to let the free individual, inspired by his personal piety, make his own decision on the meaning of the Law. The Pharisees, anxious to protect the bodily existence of Israel, believed themselves obliged to hold fast to the impersonal authority of the Law. They chose rather to pronounce every part of it, all exactions of the tribal ritual as binding, than to give emphasis to its ethical, widely human principles. The conflict centered on the opposition of idea to personality, of transcendent revelation to human judgment. It arose from questions like the one related in Mark 3:1-6. Is it allowed to break the Sabbath rule in order to help your fellow man? The Pharisees, in holding to the letter

[6] ". . . both Jesus and the Pharisees shared in common a Judaism expressed in the terms of a spiritual Theism, developed in the Synagogue and the home, and learned there alike by the Pharisees and by Jesus. . . . It was the spiritual inheritance of the Jew into which he entered by natural piety, and from which neither the simple and unlearned nor the Scribe versed in the subtleties of the Halachah was excluded." The teachings of the Sermon on the Mount and even the Lord's Prayer were familiar to the Pharisees: ". . . in regard to these fundamental beliefs there was no disagreement between Jesus and the Pharisees." Robert Travers Herford, *Pharisaism, Its Aim and Its Method* (New York, 1912), pp. 126 ff., and p. 119.

of the Law, maintained that no deviation was permissible except in the case of extreme emergency, that is, of danger to life. They held that whatever could be delayed to another day, should be left undone on the Sabbath. Jesus interpreted the Law in a more liberal way, contending that any help of an essential order could be administered, regardless of the Sabbath.

Jesus did not question the authority of the Law. He observed the decrees of the ritual, however freely he interpreted some points of it.[7] So did the first evangelical community; when Peter was in Antioch he strongly objected to Paul's sitting down to table with the heathen. On the other hand, one is entitled to say that the Pharisees themselves, in their way, defended the spiritual element in Jewish religion by refusing to let any human being interfere with the suprahuman authority of the Law.

Anyway, this was an internal Jewish conflict, and the teachings of Jesus himself prescribed a Judaism as genuine as that of the former Jewish prophets. The break with Judaism, the break with the Law, was not effected by Jesus, but by Paul. He became the actual founder of the Christian Church when he opened the community of Jesus to the whole flood of pagan cults and ideas.

In the teachings of Jesus there is nothing to which Jews could not subscribe. What the Jews could not accept was the later belief in the incarnation of God, and the dogma that Jesus was the Divine redeemer who by his martyrdom took the burden of salvation from the shoulders of men once and for all. The Jews were to carry on this burden and the responsibility for the human condition; they could not consider themselves redeemed, and relieved of the lasting task of working, every single one of them, for a brotherly world on earth. They could not be relieved because the propensity toward the fulfillment of this task

[7] "Think not that I am come to destroy the law, or the prophets: I am not come to destroy, but to fulfill." (Matthew 5:17)

was inherent in their existence; it was a living, perpetual impulse in them. Inasmuch as people are genuine Jews, really good Jews, they are in fact Christian by nature, not by a sacramental act. And therefore they could not in the past, any more than they can today, truly be converted into Christians.

But saying this, I do not mean to overrate the Jewish people. We all know very well that the Jews are no model human beings, and that we have, as all peoples have, ugly spots on our history and on our people. What I mean to say is simply this: that the genuine Christian trend is indeed a genuine Jewish trend, which pervades all of Jewish history, from the prophets and the Essenes and Jesus, who emerged from the prophetic tradition, through the martyrdom of many centuries, and the ever-recurrent surge of this Christian impulse in close Jewish circles, as for instance the cabbalistic "Sages of the Heart" in the thirteenth and in the sixteenth century, and the Polish and Russian Hasidim in the eighteenth century, to the marked dedication of modern Jews to pacifist and socialist aims. I do not know of any other people who possess in their revered writings a declaration like this, set down in a Midrash: "Any distress concerning Israel and the people of the world is a distress. Any distress concerning Israel alone is no distress."

The intense hatred of Christendom toward the Jews, passing through many phases, has manifested itself in various forms. It can, however, be traced back ultimately to one fundamental motivation: the resistance and resentment of residual paganism, even under the aegis of the Christian Churches, against actual and activated universality. Paganism is essentially the primeval, ineradicable clinging to particularity, to phenomenal multifariousness and variegation, to the immediately gratifying and reassuring life of the senses. The pervading theme of the Old Testament, on the other hand, is the long and hard struggle of the inner core of Israel to establish the prevalence of the principle of unity and universality over the drives of particularity and multiplicity, the prevalence of the one omnipresent God over the many local deities, of the spirit over the senses, of legality over self-righteousness.

The foundation of the Christian world religion was made possible by Paul's introducing of pagan cults and concepts into the Jewish religion, and that meant in the end surrendering original Christianity—that is, the teachings of the prophets and Jesus, to ecclesiastical Christology. Hence, Christian hostility against the Jews perpetuated the two great resentments of ancient paganism, which grew stronger and stronger and finally formed a huge, world-wide line of battle against Judaism. The first of these resentments derived from the pagan aversion to the wholly spiritual Jewish God, Who refuses localization, mediation, representation, let alone incarnation; in short, all appeal to the senses. The abstract nature of the God of Israel was further emphasized by His intransigent law that was to be imposed on human life. The other resentment was directed against the arrogant, paradoxical presumption that this law claiming universality had proceeded from a particular tribe—and even included inveterate ritual particularities. This part of gentile animosity was in fact stirred up and incited ever more by the Christian Church in its efforts to distance itself from an ancestry it would never be able to disown.

The religious anti-Judaism broadened into an *economic* one when, as a result of ecclesiastical persecution, the Jews in the Middle Ages were shut off from practically all professions except small money-lending, a situation, not of their own making, which brought upon them the reputation of usurers. This accusation, however, is one of the most striking of historical paradoxes. For the Jewish prohibition of interest, as expressed in Exodus 22:25 and Leviticus 25:36-37, in the Psalms, by Ezekiel, by Jesus, and most strictly in the Talmud, stands out as an exception in the ancient world, and it is the source of the Christian pro-

hibition of interest, which was enjoined on the faithful by
Saint Jerome, a Father of the Church, and doctrinally valid
throughout the Middle Ages.

After the Jews had emerged from the medieval ordeals of
massacres, stakes, expulsions, ghetto life and civil degradation, a *social* discrimination persisted under the cover of
civil rights. This social anti-Judaism eventually developed
into a *racial* one, that is, into anti-Semitism. And when we
examine the arguments raised against the Jews by modern
anti-Semites, we find again the crucial point to be the
specific Jewish combination of universality and particularity; the connection of Jewish internationality with the survival as a special folk group; the claim to be citizens of
modern nation-states and citizens of the modern world,
while at the same time remaining Jews, sometimes down to
the observance of that strange, atavistic tribal ritual, as it
is preserved in Jewish Orthodoxy. This very connection, en-
compassing the most detached supranational, often antinational, humanism and the most restrictive religious paro-
chialism, fomented the absurd legend of a Jewish world
conspiracy aiming at a racial domination of the world.

After this survey we are finally in a position to attempt an
answer to the questions that are put before us.

I have characterized the Jews as a tribe directed toward
humanity at large. This makes for an essentially dynamic,
essentially historical, existence, an existence constantly in
process, in the process of sublimation, of transforming and
translating parochial forms into universal ones. We may see
God from two angles, as the personal creator and ruler of
the universe, or as the spiritual projection of an ultimate
aiming at the universe, inherent in the Jewish people. In
any case, the affirmation of the *uni-verse*, in the most literal
sense of the word, is the basic Jewish feature that runs
through all stages of Israel and that links the residue of
primordial times, the Orthodox Jew, with Einstein. It is

this feature for which we stand and suffer, a feature so topical at this moment that, we may say, our time has come only now. The entire world appears to be moving into the focus of this issue.

Let us look now at the burning questions. The question whether we should become Christian has been answered. What distinguishes Judaism from Christianism is not Christianity, but Christology, an issue on which Christian denominations themselves differ among each other. And whether Jews become Catholic, or Lutheran, or Presbyterian, does not, particularly in our time, affect the situation of Judaism, or of the world. What we hold, in contrast to the Christian Churches' emphasis on the personal cult, is best expressed by an old rabbinical interpretation: "God says 'Would that you forget my name, but follow in my ways!'"

Can we be good Jews and at the same time good Americans? I think we can, insofar as we are not supposed to serve a narrow nationalism, and to follow this country into its errors and its wrongs. We shall never subscribe to this abominable maxim; "my country—right or wrong" nor, of course, "my tribe—right or wrong." We are bound to be human beings first, and to lead our fellow men to this profession above all professions and confessions. But since we have reached a stage of history where the good of any particular nation begins to coincide with the good of humanity at large, the general line of conduct demanded of us as Jews, as Americans, and as citizens of our world, is practically the same—there is no conflict.

We may, of course, likewise be good nationals of the State of Israel. But what I would insist on is that the Israeli nationality is not identical with our quality and existence as Jews. I am all for support of the State of Israel: we need it as a haven and as a cultural center; we admire, and are gratefully proud of its achievements. But I refuse to agree that the State of Israel and the Israeli nation should be considered as the ultimate aim and end of the Jewish career. We are forever, I think, less and more than a nation; we have different and older origins, and we have different and higher aims. Our existence as a nation can of necessity be only a restricted and transitory one, a sector and a stage of Jewish history. Apart from the fact that the State of Israel is unlikely ever to be capable of absorbing so much as the nine million Jews who survived the Nazi onslaught, it cannot be that the end of our endurance through thousands of years is our homecoming in itself: that we should be confined within a tiny statehood, participating in that competition of sanctified egoisms which modern nations keep enacting before our eyes. Israel will never achieve the numerical and material power to be fit for this sort of competition, especially now when the protagonists of this sinister spectacle are giants of continental proportions. And after all, it seems somewhat late for such a national aspiration, when we all hope to see, when it is in fact our last and only hope to see, the end of unlimited national sovereignty, and the dawn of a united humanity.

No, I do not think that we should, after having held out through the history of man, give up the intrinsic aims to which the Jewish people were originally dedicated. I believe, on the contrary, that we have today an intensified responsibility in respect of these aims. I believe that, in whatever country we have a part, America, Russia, or Israel, we are committed to take the dangerous stand for peace and for a united humanity, for a new order of social and economic as well as political democracy.

I have no quarrel with our universalists if only they were a little more conscious of the immeasurable support that our Jewish tradition can afford us in our striving for the common goal. And it is for this reason, not for the sake of national self-glorification, that I believe we should not discard our Judaism before the great task is fulfilled. But if ever this horrible nightmare of national and ideological rivalries, of mutual hatred and destruction, may end, if a time comes when men of all breeds and creeds may agree to be nothing else than brotherly human beings—then we also, indeed we before all, will gladly cease to be Jews.

The Jews in Europe

IN THIS present age that has seen Jewry receive from the Nazis the dreadful and dubious accolade of being proclaimed the archfiend of mankind, in an enterprise which all but wrecked the world, it is hard to imagine that the Jews were ever a people just like any other. Hard, too, because the Jews, for better or for worse, have come to be taken by all peoples as the quintessence of political and social abnormality. And yet once upon a time, in remote antiquity, they were, like other ethnic communities, a people with their own lands, their own kingdom, their own native religion, one among many other peoples, kingdoms and religions. Their kingdom perished, however, for it could not withstand the onslaught of the much more powerful empires which then succeeded one another, the Babylonian, Persian, Greek and eventually the Roman Empire. But the people and their religion—and this is where the abnormality begins—did not perish with the kingdom, but surived for thousands of years; indeed, as the kingdom waned, the religion became steadily more powerful and eventually begot that world-wide new religion which has become the cupola of European and Western civilization.

When the Jews in the pre-Christian era first stepped upon the soil of Europe, they came in much the same circumstances as did members of other Mediterranean peoples. Like them, they were either sold as slaves, or had fled from

31

the conquerors of their own country, or came as traders or diplomatic emissaries. Their customs and their cult were but one more hue in the many-colored pagan world.

But soon they began to distinguish themselves by one unique quality, which was the origin of all their other differences. Unconverted and unsubmerged, through all that befell them they held fast to their religion—and since at that time religion meant, not just a creed, but the very way of life of the people, this implied at the same time holding fast also to a host of specific customs and observances. One may approve or disapprove of this quality, this quasi-biological and intellectual obstinacy, one may regard it as peerless steadfastness or historical arrogance— one thing is certain, and that is that without this quality there would have been no Christianity and no Christian civilization. When Alexander's conquering armies broke down the barriers between Greece, which at that time represented Europe, and the Asian and African Orient, there followed a great intermingling of religions and peoples. What saved the Judaeo-Christian idea from total absorption in the pagan world was that selfsame obstinacy in the name of which European Christians later persecuted the Jews.

The history of the Jews in Europe is the history of the growth of their abnormality and its transformation from a spontaneous and voluntary attitude into an involuntary, enforced one.

Jewish immigration into Europe took place in several waves, which, as in a rising tide, overlapped each other and steadily spread to higher latitudes, until there were more or less dense settlements of Jews throughout the whole of Europe. Under the pressure of constant harassment, the flow of immigration kept moving on through migrations within the Continent.

The first wave of immigration, which began in the centuries before Christ, carried the Jews only into Europe's southern latitudes, into the Mediterranean regions which were then the sole civilized ones. They came to the great peninsulas of Greece, Italy and Spain—and, in the natural way of historical development, first to the lands that were nearest to Asia, that is, to Greece and the neighboring areas on the Black Sea.

The presence of Jews in Greece is attested by inscriptions dating from as early as the first half of the second century B.C. These first Greek Jews were probably prisoners from the Maccabean wars (170-140 B.C.), that Judaic rebellion against the domination of the Syrian dynasty of Seleucus, one of Alexander's governors; they were no doubt brought to Greece originally by slave traders and were later freed. Subsequently, after Pompey had conquered the whole of Greek Asia and had united it with European Greece under Roman dominion (64-63 B.C.), their numbers were swelled by the arrival of Greek-speaking Jews from Hellenistic Asia Minor and the islands, who had taken refuge there from earlier calamities in Palestine. Spreading out from the Greek areas in the wake of Greek colonization, the Jews settled on the shores of the Bosporus and on the northern coast of the Black Sea, on the estuaries of the Dniester, Dnieper and Bug, in the Crimea and the Caucasus. Like the Greeks they came as traders, bartered Asian manufactures for corn and salt, and founded their emporia and communities in the prospering Greek city republics of those parts and in the Crimean kingdom of Bosporus.

Not much later than in Greece, Jewish settlements made their appearance in Italy as well, but it was not until the middle of the first century B.C. that the community in Rome became of some importance. Once again, this development seems to have begun with prisoners, but prisoners, this time, whom Pompey carried away after the conquest of Jerusalem (63 B.C.). Some of these prisoners were ransomed by their people in Judaea; others, who had been allotted as slaves

to Romans, were soon released by the latter, because their
observance of the Sabbath and of other religious commandments, which at that time their masters respected, greatly
impaired the Jews' usefulness as slaves. But they stayed on
in Rome and settled on the far side of the Tiber, in Traste-
vere, the location of the market for overseas merchandise
shipped to Rome by Greek sailors; the district was inhab-
ited mostly by small shopkeepers and artisans, emancipated
slaves and suchlike lesser folk. Gradually the whole district
became one continuous Jewish quarter, although Jews later
settled also in other parts of the town. This community was
quite sizeable even in the time of Caesar and Augustus, and
received strong reinforcements after the destruction of
Jerusalem by Titus (A.D. 70), when the process of settlement
by prisoners repeated itself on a larger scale.

But immigration was not the sole reason for the rapid
growth of Jewish communities in Europe. There was another, more significant reason of much wider consequence.
This was that Judaism was the first proselytizing religion,
the first religion with a mission not only for its own tribe
but for all peoples, the first whose god, according to Isaiah
49:6, expressly gave the people of Israel "for a light to the
Gentiles, that thou mayest be my salvation unto the end
of the earth." Certainly, the Jews' proselytizing was not
nearly as active and organized a missionary activity as to
make it comparable with that of the Christians. It rested
mainly on the example of an all-embracing and extremely
rigid divine worship and on the very concept of the Jewish
god himself, the one and only god lacking all the personal
and sensory attributes of the pagan gods, the god without
mythology, without name, without image. He was not just
another god, he was another kind of god, almost impersonal
and, from the point of view of the pagans, hardly a god at
all, but rather a principle or an idea. That is why Greek
writers called the Jews "a tribe of philosophers." One
would have thought that so sober and abstract a conception

of God would not have had much attraction for men of
other nations. But it seems that in that age of transition, at
that time of wild and confused multiplicity of intermingling
mystery cults, the very clarity of the Jewish religion, its ra-
tionality and moral strictness made an extraordinary impression upon the pagans, especially since this religion was
attested by revelation and commanded the unshakeable con-
victions of its adherents. In any event, it seems that more
than a few were converted to Judaism at that time; "the
customs of this criminal people," the Roman writer Seneca
complained, "are gaining so much ground that they find
followers in all countries, and thus the defeated have imposed their law upon the victors" (*victi victoribus leges
dederunt*).

Not all the proselytes, it is true, could bring themselves
to accept the more unusual prescriptions of the Jewish
ritual, and in time all Jewish communities came to be sur-
rounded by a fringe of so-called "God-worshippers," semi-
proselytes, who, while confessing to the spiritual God of
Israel and His ethical commandments, did not feel bound
by the ritual. It was mainly among these people that the
Christian doctrine first took root, and they became the
core of the first Christian communities. Wherever Paul
the Apostle turned on his missionary journeys, he found
established Jewish settlements with their fringe of "God-
worshipping" pagans; he preached in the synagogues of
Thessalonica, of Athens and Corinth (Acts 16-18), and his
intention of going from Rome to Spain suggests that that
country, too, had its fully developed Jewish communities at
the beginning of the Christian era. In outward things as
well, therefore, Judaism paved the way for Christianity and
laid the foundations for the latter's spread in Europe.

The next wave of expansion, which gathered force and
significance during the early Christian centuries, carried
the Jews to more northerly regions, to northern Italy, Gaul,

and what was then Germania. At the same time the Jewish
settlements in the South became denser and more powerful.
New immigrants from Asia and Africa, fugitives and
traders alike, kept streaming into the completely accessible
Mediterranean Basin, for Europe was the America of the
declining world of antiquity. And the status of the Jews
had risen. Thanks to their wide distribution on all the
shores of the Mediterranean and to the close coherence
of their Diaspora, the Jews occupied a key position in the
economy of Roman Byzantium during the fourth century,
for they were the ideal intermediaries in the flourishing
trade between Byzantium and the great Jewish center of
Alexandria, and as such quite indispensable. They were
great merchants and shipowners, but they were also silk
manufacturers, farmers, lawyers and, above all, physicians.
The heads of Jewish communities were at the same time
ephors, that is, the chief magistrates of the Jewish quarters
of the town. During the same period Jews held high civic
office in southern Italy, in Apulia and Calabria. Here they
specialized, almost to the point of monopoly, in dyeing
cloth and manufacturing silk piecegoods; in Sicily, they
were date growers. They also were famed as goldsmiths.
Apart from their unshakeable loyalty to the commandments
and customs of their religion, they were thoroughly Hellen-
ized and Latinized; the Jewish, and often Hebrew, tomb
inscriptions of that time display nothing but Greek and
Roman names.

The Italian and Byzantine Jews formed a unified cultural
group and as such a bridge between the numerous con-
verging civilizations. They spoke Italian in northern Italy,
Greek in the Balkans, and Greek or Arabic in Byzantine
southern Italy, but they all had the common tie of the
Hebrew revival. For this region became the first spiritual
center of European Jewry, the first major station on the
road of the spirit of Judaism from the Orient to the North.
Midrashim were written here, expositions which developed

the scriptures through narrative and ethical interpretation, as well as sacred hymns and the first Jewish philosophy in Europe—a work of religious philosophy by Shabbethai Donnolo, a man well versed in astronomy, astrology and medicine, who studied "the books of the Greeks and Arabs, the wisdom of the Chaldaeans and Indians," and who was personal physician to the Byzantine governor of Calabria.

Very early, when Rome was still a republic, the Greek colonization of the French Mediterranean coast—Marseille was originally a Greek colony—had brought Jewish emigrants in its train. From there Jewish settlements spread throughout the whole of southern Gaul to Narbonne, Arles, Avignon, Bordeaux, etc., and in that pagan age the native Celts, Romans, Greeks and Jews all lived peacefully together in this Roman province. This province, today's Provence, was to become one of the most important centers of European Jewry. It is the only spot in France where Jews have lived without interruption, through all persecutions and expulsions.

The Jewish emigrants from the regions of the Eastern, Hellenistic Diaspora were followed by Jewish merchants from Italy. These latter carried their trade into northern Gaul and, along the Roman roads, to the banks of the Rhine. In Roman Cologne (*Colonia Agrippina*), there was a Jewish settlement before there were Germans. The first Christian emperor, Constantine, gave orders that the wealthier members of the Jewish community at Cologne were to be drafted into municipal service, the kind of jobs that no one liked taking on at that time, because they entailed great responsibilities and expenses.

In pagan times, therefore, the position of the Jews was outwardly still quite normal. Some outbreaks of violence against them did, it is true, occur in Hellenistic Alexandria, and there is no lack of hostile remarks in Roman literature. All this was directed against the Jews' strict adherence to their Law and their religious customs, especially the dietary rules and the observance of the Sabbath day of rest, which caused the Jews to isolate themselves to some extent from their pagan surroundings. But it was also directed against the Jews' independent spirit, against their stubborn defense of their Palestinian land and their sacred shrines. They were the only oriental people who again and again put up a violent resistance to Roman rule. However, there was no discriminatory legislation against Jews in the pre-Christian Roman Empire, and in A.D. 212 the Emperor Caracalla conferred Roman citizenship upon them as upon all other inhabitants of the Empire. If anything, they even received more favorable treatment than the Christians, who deployed a much more active and dangerous propaganda and eventually won out against paganism.

This victory, confirmed by the conversion to Christianity of Emperor Constantine and by the giving of legal status to the dogma of Christ's divine nature in A.D. 325, made that date a tragic one for Jewry. For from that moment onward the European Jews became an abnormality in the body politic of the nations, a persisting, universal minority, and a minority of a very special kind at that, since it expressed ethnic community through religion and religion through the people's way of life. European paganism was gradually absorbed by Christianity, but Judaism was not pagan, it was the womb of Christianity, to which it was indissolubly joined through the latter's physical and spiritual origin and Christ's own undeniable loyalty to the Jewish God and Jewish Law. Christianity was therefore forced to fight Judasim while acknowledging its own link with it, and used this very link as a weapon against the Jews. They alone were made to bear the full guilt of Christ's crucifixion, while the Romans, who after all had a not unimportant part in it, but became converts, were studiously exonerated. It was the Jews who became God's murderers, the witnesses and instruments of Christ's sacrifice, and their allegedly predestined and ordained delusion, which was supposed to have blinded them so that they did not recognize Jesus as the Messiah and the Son of God, made them disgraced outcasts. God, wrote St. Augustine, had set the mark of Cain upon the Jews, "lest any finding them should kill them." They should not be destroyed, therefore, but preserved, and preserved as the "witnesses of their guilt and of our truth," servants to Christian peoples forever. This view determined the fate of European Jews until modern times, and only from this point of departure can their fate be rightly understood. All the restrictions and the persecutions, all the martyrdom that Christians had suffered at the hands of pagan Romans, the Christians now meted out to the Jews.

In its early period, Christianity had undergone the same ordeal that was to be Judaism's throughout its history. The Christians were accused of having no god and hating men, of setting themselves apart from the non-Christian community, of being unpatriotic, indifferent toward the state, arrogantly intolerant of all the pleasures of life, and of mocking all that was sacred to millions of people. They were a prey to the caprice of whatever ruler happened to be in power, as well as to the passions of the crowd, who held them responsible for every public misfortune because their rituals were supposed to have angered the gods. The most fantastic conspiracies and crimes were attributed to them. "When the Tiber overflowed its banks, when the heavens remained close and rainless, when the earth trembled, when famine broke out, at once everyone cried: 'Throw the Christians to the lions!' " (Tertullian, *Apologeticus* 40) In those days it was the Christians who were accused of ritual murder, and the charge was believed even by enlightened men like Tacitus and Pliny, just as the protocols of the Elders of Zion were believed in our days. With the spread of Christianity, the influence of pagan elements on it increased and drew it away from its Jewish origins. In this way the Christian Church began its fundamental struggle against the Jews, and in imposing upon

them all that Christians had suffered earlier, it did not occur
to the latter to follow the old biblical admonition to "love
the stranger as thyself, for ye were strangers in the land
of Egypt."

The process which led from there to the ghetto and
ultimately to Hitler was, of course, a very gradual and
complex one, subject to many fluctuations and more than
one interruption. But the guidelines for the treatment of
Jews were laid down very early: first, the suppression of the
Jewish religion and the prohibition on the building of
new synagogues (Council of Laodicea, between 343 and
380); then the prohibition of intermarriage between Jews
and Christians (under Emperor Constantius II, 337-361);
the prohibition on Jews keeping Christian slaves, which
later evolved into the canon law according to which no
Jew must be given any sort of power over Christians, since
Jews were forever to be the servants of Christians; and
finally the exclusion of Jews from all public office and the
restriction of their civil rights by Theodosius II (408-450)—
the first step to the complete outlawing of the Jews. But it
was a long time yet before Catholic Christianity had so
thoroughly pervaded the peoples of Europe that these rules
could really become effective, and even then their sway
was occasionally limited by practical necessity.

The period of the migration of the German tribes now set
in. The western Roman Empire collapsed and the German
tribes flooded into the Roman provinces. They did not,
as such, display any hostility toward the Jews, and indeed
those who first adopted Aryan Christianity (so named after
Bishop Arius, who denied that Christ was the Son of God)
continued after their conversion to keep on the best of
terms with the Jews. Jewish communities, for instance,
prospered in the north Italian towns under the rule of the
Aryan Ostrogoths and Lombards, whose kings granted the
Jews autonomy and full freedom of occupation and pro-

tected them against the violent attacks of the Catholic clergy, who did their best to incite the people against the Jews. In their turn, the Jews fought side by side with the Ostrogoths against the armies of the Byzantine emperor, from whose religious fanaticism they could expect nothing good, and in Provence they battled with the Aryan Visigoths against the Catholic Franks.

But Aryan Christianity was defeated by the Nicene creed, which the ruling churches of Rome and Byzantium recognized as the lawful Christian dogma. This dogma, which proclaims the essential divinity of Christ, was necessarily in the sharpest opposition to Judaism. All religious groups which denied the divine nature of Christ, or which merely assumed some difference of substance between God the Father, the Old Testament God, and Christ, or inclined through some doctrine toward the Old Testament, all these groups were henceforth branded not only as heretics, but first and invariably also as "Judaisers." Usually, this had the direst consequences for the Jews themselves. It happened in the case of the Byzantine iconoclasts, who rejected the cult of saints' images; it happened with the heretic sects of the thirteenth century, and happened again with the Reformation.

By and by all the rulers and, with them, all the nations of Western Europe, adopted the Nicene creed, the Catholic faith. Besides, in this disturbed age of anarchy and shifting power the Catholic Church with its ubiquitous organization was the only stable authority. It was the enduring vestige of Roman government, its bishops guided the hesitant minds of the barbarian rulers, who were hardly familiar as yet with the tasks of orderly public administration. Thus the Church gained an overwhelming influence, and the councils of bishops and metropolitans assumed the role of legislative bodies. But however often these councils re-emphasized the condemnation of Judaism and enjoined the nations to apply the above-mentioned measures for the suppression and forcible conversion of the Jews, and however much zealous priests kept preaching against the Jews, however relentlessly and violently they did so, these measures were in practice applied only sporadically and incompletely. The kings were only too glad to avail themselves of the Jews not only as merchants and financial agents, but also as personal physicians and diplomatic negotiators, or indeed, like Chilperic the Merovingian, as advisers in important matters of state. Wherever clerical zeal did not interfere, the Christian population lived in peace and friendship with the Jews. Here and there even Church dignitaries were glad to frequent Jews and found arguments to excuse themselves. In 472, for example, the Bishop of Clermont recommended his Jewish agent to the Bishop of Tournay with the justification that it was all wrong to forgo the services of a Jew, if only for the very good reason that as long as he lived he could, after all, still be converted to the true faith. Besides, the Bishop attested, these people were wont to conduct their business honestly, and therefore it was quite all right to befriend them, even though one had to condemn their unbelief. The multiplication of specific interdictions makes it clear that Jews held state office, that they farmed the taxes, were shipowners and owned large landed estates with all the rights of a lord of the manor and seignior. "Beset with grief and fearful unto death," Pope Stephen III wrote to the Bishop of Narbonne (between 768 and 772), because "the Jews own allods [heritable estates free of any feudal rent] on Christian soil and on fully equal terms with Christians, thanks to the privileges granted them by the Frankish kings. Christians are cultivating Jewish vineyards and fields!" At that time, Judaism and Christianity were even still in missionary competition: religious disputations were arranged, in which the Jews with their rational arguments often carried the day, and Christians came to the synagogue to listen to the sermons. Nor were mixed marriages and conversions to Judaism at all rare. Even high clerics, such as the confessor of Emperor Louis the Pious, went over to Judaism. In consequence, the anti-Jewish propaganda of the Church became all the more violent. The first local expulsions of Jews took place around that time.

In the Carolingian Empire and in Spain the status of the Jews was rising. Charlemagne was the first independent and outstanding ruler among the Germanic kings. While he spent a great deal of believer's energy on promoting Christianity, of whose civilizing power he was well aware, he kept astonishingly free of the influence of the Church— so much so that under his rule there began a premature movement of enlightenment and rationalism. He resisted the clergy's demands that he should restrict the Jews' right to own land and should forbid them to employ Christian laborers. At that time the Jews were the driving force in world trade, because of their connections in Asia and Africa, their education and knowledge of languages. Their prominence in this field is borne out by the standing clause in Charlemagne's capitularies and indeed by much later ordinances: "Jews and other merchants. . . ." Jews were the pioneers of trade in the newly won barbarian regions of Germany, just as subsequently they were indispensable wherever a barter economy was to be transformed into a money economy. Jewish settlements at that time were spreading to the newly founded German cities, well into Bavaria and Saxony. But large-scale trade was beginning to be a matter of international politics, especially in relations with the Orient. Thus Jews were Charlemagne's envoys to the Caliph of Baghdad (797-802). Charlemagne seems even to have been a patron of Jewish learning, since it is said that he prevailed upon the Baghdad scholar Machir to come to Narbonne and thus founded the first Talmudic school in southern France.

Under Charlemagne's son, Louis the Pious (814-840), the Jews were still in a favorable position, but the attacks of the Church were mounting ominously. Not that this Emperor allowed himself to be intimidated either; not even the aforementioned conversion of his confessor led him to sacrifice the Jews. But precisely in order to help them, he inaugurated a questionable arrangement: the imperial protection of the Jews. This meant not only confirmation of their exclusion from the general civic order, but also the first step in a process by which, in time, the Jews came to live throughout Europe in bondage to the rulers and powerful lords.

Two events were decisive for the coming doom of the Jews: the establishment of the feudal system and the advance of Islam into Europe, which incited the Christians to the Crusades.

The rising feudal lords began their struggle for power by dispossessing the already vulnerable Jews of landed property. All they had to do to this end was to ally themselves with the Church and to invoke the canon law which forbade the Jews to keep Christian dependents. The application of this prohibition made farming impossible for the Jews and ruled out their incorporation in the feudal system. In any event, the feudal order was so permeated with Christian forms and ideas that for this reason alone Jews could be no part of it. The rest was done by the mass fanaticism of the Crusades, which spread and consolidated among the peoples of Europe the sort of animosity against the Jews which hitherto had been limited to the clergy and to sporadic and transitory outbreaks of mob violence.

The origin of the Crusades can be traced back to the Arab invasion of Spain and the unrest which the Arabs' initially irresistible advance caused in Christian Europe. Having crossed over from North Africa, the Arabs had cleared the Visigoths from the whole Pyrenean peninsula except for a small area on the northwest coast (the modern Galicia and Asturia).

As long as the Spanish Visigoths were Aryans, they lived

in untroubled amity with the Jews, whose communities were their militant outposts against the Catholic Franks in the North, in Provence, and against Byzantine power in Africa in the South. But when, around the year 600, the Visigoths became Catholics, things changed radically, all the more so as the Roman Church in Spain distinguished itself right from the outset by its particularly ardent and aggressive religious zeal. It quickly succeeded in enforcing its compulsory anti-Jewish measures, and by 613 the Jews were left only with the choice between conversion and expulsion. Some of them, especially farmers who did not want to give up their land, became the first to find a way out in marranism, the public acceptance of Christianity combined with private fidelity to the faith and rites of Judaism. This phenomenon did not by any means remain limited to Spain; but whenever the crushing pressure lifted slightly, the marranos openly returned to Judaism.

Small wonder that the Jews supported the Moslems who in 711 invaded Spain from North Africa, which they had conquered in the meantime. The almost eight centuries of Moslem rule in Spain were by and large one of the most brilliant periods of European Jewry. Though occasionally the Jews had to suffer from the intolerance of the Mohammedan clergy, this was nothing compared with the hatred of the Christian Church, nor did they suffer as much as the Christians themselves, who under the Arabs were forced into a marranism of their own and who, as landowners, were completely ruined by an Islamic law which freed the bondsmen of Christians. Under the Arabs, Jews rose to the highest positions, sometimes ruling the land as all-powerful ministers and viziers. Their communities became flourishing cultural centers. whose scholars and poets rivaled the Arabs in philosophy and science. Outstanding among the multitude of great Jews of the time, who sometimes wrote in Arabic and translated from Greek and Hebrew into Arabic, were Hasdai ibn Shaprut

(915-970), the adviser of the caliph Abdurrahman III, a polymath who fostered alike Jewish theology and the profane sciences, especially astronomy and medicine; Solomon ibn Gabirol (c.1021-c.1070), known in Arabic as Avicebron, a poet and philosopher whose theories influenced Christian scholastics, especially Duns Scotus; Moses Maimonides (1135-1204), the father of Jewish rationalism, who made Aristotelian philosophy available to the Jewish tradition; and finally the great Hebrew poet Judah Halevi (c.1085-c.1140). But Spain was not only the cradle of Jewish enlightenment, but also of its extreme contrast, Jewish mysticism, which here found authoritative expression in the *Zohar*, the Book of Brilliance—an impressive compilation and philosophical elaboration of old traditional materials published by Moses de Leon toward the end of the thirteenth century. It is a commentary on the Pentateuch from a mystical point of view, which incorporates elements of Neo-Platonic philosophy in Judaism; with it, the second mainstream of Jewish tradition, the Kabbala (which means reception, received by tradition) rose to become the peer and rival of the Talmud. The Spanish-Jewish thinkers were of decisive significance for European learning, for it was largely they who handed on to posterity the works of the Greek philosophers, especially Aristotle; these long-lost writings, which had reappeared among the Islamic scholars of Asia Minor, now found their way via North Africa and Spain to Christian scholasticism, where they generated the first stirrings of modern rational thought and science.

The high position occupied by the Jews in the Arab states had the consequence that Christian rulers in Spain, the descendants of the Visigoth persecutors of the Jews, also used Jews as diplomats and ministers, and as mediators between different civilizations. The middle of the twelfth century indeed witnessed a complete reversal of the former relationships. In the same year as the French and German crusaders set forth to conquer Jerusalem, Moslem Spain was

invaded from Africa by the militantly fanatical Mohammedan Almohades, who overturned the more moderate Almor-
avides, sacked the synagogues and forced many Jews into
Islamic marranism; but many others, who refused to
capitulate, fled northward into Christian Castile.

This was the time of gathering doom for Jewry throughout
Europe. Both real and imaginary persecutions of Christians
in the Moslem countries, especially in Palestine whither
Christian pilgrims flocked in increasing numbers, induced
the Church to summon the princes and peoples of Europe
to arms against the infidels, to reconquer the Holy Land.
The Church took advantage of this great opportunity to
enlarge its influence upon the nations and to implant it in-
eradicably in people's minds. The clergy and the monks
brought their rabble-rousing to the boiling point. Not only
lords and knights, but peasants, townsmen and men greedy
for adventure and booty gathered for the Crusades. But
even before the expeditions were properly organized, un-
disciplined mobs in France and Germany launched out
against the local infidels—that is, the Jews. They assaulted
the old Jewish communities at Rouen, and then in the
Rhineland cities of Trier, Cologne, Mainz, Speyer and
Worms, they burnt and plundered and massacred all Jews
who refused baptism. Many Jews committed suicide rather than fall into the hands of the mob. Here and there the
feudal and city lords, the bishops and the princes, who
needed the Jews very much for economic reasons and indeed had attracted them with special privileges, tried to
protect them and gave them refuge in their own palaces.
But with few exceptions they were not steadfast and cour-
ageous enough to withstand the crowds who beleaguered
the palaces. Often they exacted a heavy price from the
Jews for this ineffective protection. To be sure, there were
true Christians, like Bernard of Clairvaux, who were
shocked at these outrages and tried their best to counter

them, but mass hysteria was unleashed, and it took a very long time to subdue the storm of massacres of the Jews, which during the Crusades swept across the whole of Western and Central Europe.

When at last it spent itself, European Jewry found itself in a radically changed position. Only now, from the twelfth and thirteenth centuries onward, were the Jews truly defenseless, at the mercy of whatever powers wished to exploit them for whatever purposes. For only now—and this is the decisive point—only now had the Jews lost their ground, the basis of their existence among the European nations. The Mohammedans were far away, the wars against them were slowly ebbing and being replaced by peaceful commercial and cultural exchange. But the Jews were right there in the country, and it was upon them that the spirit of the Crusades now fastened in perpetuity. Centuries of incitement to hatred against the infidels, of rousing every available superstition among the masses, had so deeply implanted hostility against the Jews and distrust of them in the unconscious depths of the human mind, that down to our day no amount of enlightenment, no reasonable argument, no factual evidence succeeded in eradicating this attitude. The effect of the Crusades is a lesson in what propaganda can achieve with people.

From then on there existed no crime, no public misfortune and no magic of which the Jews were not held capable and indeed responsible. In 1171 the accusation of Jewish ritual murder made its appearance at Blois, in France; by ritual command, it was said, the Jews had to partake of Christian blood on the feast of the Passover, and the unleavened bread was baked with Christian blood. This accusation had first been leveled in pagan Rome against the Christians; but in the Jewish case it was particularly absurd for the simple reason that Jewish law proscribes the consumption of blood of any kind. In the following centuries the charge was again and again disproved by emperors, kings and popes, by repeated declarations and commissions of Christian scholars—yet there were still ritual murder trials in Europe in the nineteenth and twentieth centuries, before Hitler. If some epidemic broke out, the Jews were supposed to have poisoned the wells. And they were permanently suspect on many counts: profanation of the host, bewitching the people, poisoning the sick in their care as physicians, practicing black magic. The Devil himself seemed to be incarnate in the Jews.

Nor was this all. The Jews had not only lost their connection with the people, they were at the same time harassed economically. The feudal system and the now effective prohibition on keeping Christian servants excluded the Jews from agriculture. In any event their position was now so precarious that it deterred them from living among country folk and tying up their wealth in landed property. In the towns, the crafts had become a monopoly of the Christian guilds, which admitted no Jews and thus barred them from industry. Trade, finally, had in the meantime passed into the hands of Christians, who had no difficulty in squeezing out the Jews. There was only moneylending left, and this was virtually forced upon the Jews since Christians at that time were still forbidden to take interest by a canon law which Christianity had inherited from ancient Judaism. But this trade was as ill-famed as it was indispensable, and on top of all their other disabilities the Jews were thus accused of usury. Significantly, this charge was leveled against them first in the twelfth century, and since then has become more and more insistent. For when, later, Christians themselves took control of all high finance, the Jews were left with small-scale, local moneylending and pawnbroking, so that they always appeared to the poor folk in the obnoxious role of creditor.

After the Crusades, then, the Jews had nothing and no one to fall back on except the kings and lords who wanted money, and who shamelessly exploited the defenseless. In the Western European countries and in Italy the Jews became the highly profitable property of feudal lords and rulers, who not only owned them, but sold, leased, pawned and gave them away as presents like any kind of ordinary object, and often fought over them wildly among themselves. The princes always let the Jews prosper for a while, only to take everything away from them later through taxes, extortion and expulsion. To meet the popular mood, rulers were also in the habit of decreeing, from time to time, the annulment of all debts to Jewish creditors, though often enough the population itself got rid of its debts by pogroms. In Germany the Jews became *servi camerae,* imperial servants, which at least vouchsafed them a somewhat more stable position. But the emperors were often far away, and their protection most often came too late.

During the twelfth century Jew-baiting was still sporadic and unorganized. During the thirteenth century it was canalized into a system of legal repression and banishment from general Christian life. The creator of this system was Pope Innocent III. The thirteenth century opened with the "internal crusade" against the heretical Waldensians and Albigensians of southern France, forerunners of the Reformation, whose ideas were clearly influenced also by the Jewish movement of Enlightenment in Spain. Among them were some who called themselves "wanderers" or "circumcised ones," who openly preached a return to the Old Testament. Theirs was a rapidly expanding movement which might have spelt danger to the Church, and they were mercilessly exterminated by a crushing punitive expedition mounted against them by French nobles at the Pope's instigation. One of the results was the institution of the Inquisition, the Holy Office, which was to count among its victims numberless Jewish martyrs. In addition, a canon law of the Fourth Lateran Council in 1215 prescribed that Jews (and, incidentally, also Moslems) must wear a distinctive pointed hat and badge, so as to be recognizable at

sight; in this way it would be possible to keep an effective
watch over compliance with further segregation measures,
the ban on meals in common and sexual cohabitation, the
prohibition on Jewish physicians treating Christians, etc.
With this idea of distinctive wear the Pope emulated the
fanatical caliph, Omar II (717-720), who had imposed it on
Christians and Jews.

In 1242 Paris inaugurated the era of Talmud burnings,
which continued for centuries throughout Europe. From
the end of the thirteenth century onward German Jews
were confined by law within their residential districts,
which until then had been freely chosen settlements. Common interests and customs, family connections and the
desire to be near their temples had led Jews, like other
ethnic groups, to settle together. Mounting hostility drove
them ever closer. Jews gave up their houses in the Christian
quarters of the towns, Christians moved out of the Jewish
districts. The religious community became a town within
a town, its autonomy stiffened and turned into self-defense.
And then the Jewish quarters were shut off by walls and
gates from the Christian ones.

In Spain ghettos were established in the fourteenth century, in France in the fifteenth and in Italy only in the sixteenth and seventeenth centuries. In any event, all anti-
Jewish measures in Italy were invariably applied only temporarily and relatively less strictly than elsewhere in Europe,
for in Italy the Jews with their connections all round the
Mediterranean were economically too important and powerful. Just as in Spain they had completely permeated the
aristocracy, so the Jews in Italy sometimes rose to the highest ranks of society. The popes themselves occasionally had
Jewish financiers and personal physicians, and one pope,
Anacletus II, even came from the Jewish family of Pierleoni.

The Crusades left their mark not only on the physical
existence of the Jews, but on their spiritual life. With the
Jewish settlements, Jewish learning and poetry had spread

from Spain and Italy to more northern latitudes. A southern
French center had branched off from the Spanish one, and
the Italian influence radiated northward into France and
Germany, where the Jews had been showing great intellectual activity since the tenth century, especially in the communities of Champagne, Lorraine and the Rhineland. The
Jewish scholar Kalonymos was invited by Emperor Otto II
(973-83), whose life he had saved in a battle against the
Saracens, to come from Lucca to Mainz and there founded
a celebrated and extensive family of Talmudists, poets and
mystics. This was the origin of the flowering of Talmudic
jurisprudence and of Kabbalist-Hasidic mysticism. A Talmudic academy came into being at Mainz, whose judgments gained widespread authority, and since the Jews at
that time were largely subject to their own jurisdiction, the
law schools had far more than mere ritual significance. The
jurists Judah ben Meir (Leontin) and Gershom ben Judah
worked at Mainz; at Troyes in Champagne and later at
Worms on the Rhine we find Solomon ben Isaac (Rashi),
whose comments on the text and simplifying interpretation
made the Talmud accessible to Jewish school instruction,
which until then had been based only on the Scriptures.

Just as the Byzantine-Italian cultural center was a unit,
so too was this German-French one. As far as and beyond
the Rhine all Jews spoke only French, with occasional Hebrew expressions. In the interior of Germany they eventually got used to speaking German, and Middle High
German intermingled with Hebrew later developed—on the
pattern of the Spaniole of the Spanish Sephardim—into the
Yiddish language, which Jewish fugitives took into Poland
where it was further mixed with Slavonic linguistic
elements.

But with the persecutions and with the segregation of
the Jews from their Christian environment, their intellectual
flowering withered. The Jewish mind, previously quickened

by disputations and lively intercourse with Christian scholars, and brought into stimulating contact with current
events, grew stunted and ossified in the ghetto. The Talmud
was proscribed and burnt by Christian theologians as a
devilish book, and the high level of education and intellectualism of the Jews became just one more reason
for them to be suspected of secret magic arts by the illiter-
ate and superstitious mob. Their erudition, it was said,
served only to pervert the monks and to deflect Christians
from the path of truth. And thus Jewish studies, to the extent that they managed to survive at all, were driven underground, away from light and air.

The retreat of the Jews from the world of freedom into
the prison of the ghetto was well epitomized by the mysterious figure of a Jewish minnesinger, Sueskind von Trimberg.
It was strange enough that a Jew should in the thirteenth
century still have had access to the courts of the nobility,
and in a capacity which was otherwise reserved for knights;
more strange that he should have risked departing from the
customary subjects of love and *Frauendienst* to sing instead
songs of penitence and biblical psalms which echo the bitter
experience of Jewish life. But it is not surprising that in the
end he had to give up his minstrelsy. In one of the six
poems which have come down to us he says: "I shall shun
the court of the nobles, grow a long beard and gray hair
and from now on lead the life of the old Jews. I shall wear
a long gown and pull my hat right down over my forehead;
my gait will be humble, and my song will rarely be heard
in the castles, since the lords have withdrawn their favor
from me . . . ."

The calamities of the Crusades and the subsequent periods
set off fugitive migrations and with them the third great
wave of Jewish expansion, which to all intents and purposes
completed the spread of Jewry throughout Europe. This

wave carried the Jews to England on the one hand, and on
the other to the eastern countries, to Austria, Hungary and
Poland.

In early times only a very few Jewish traders ever made
their way to England. The first real Jewish communities can
be traced back to the invasion of William the Conqueror
(1066), who systematically settled the Jews in England
because, like many another continental prince, he needed
them to introduce a money economy. The first Jewish communities were formed at Oxford and Cambridge (1073-
1075). The next impulse came from the massacre at Rouen
(1096), and after that from the persecution of the Jews by
King Philip II (Augustus), of France (1182).

Things went the same way in England as they had everywhere else. At first, under the early Norman rulers, the Jews
were still indispensable to the country's economic mobiliza-
tion, and so they were encouraged in every way, privileged
and protected against the attacks of the Church. But soon
the Crusades cast their shadow across the Channel. Although the Jews had furnished much of the money for the
building of the great cathedrals and the noblemen's castles
as well as for the conquest of Ireland in 1170, the kings
exploited every opportunity to drain away the wealth of the
Jewish communities by means of special levies and confisca-
tions and made their life unbearable. It was in England, at
Norwich in 1148, that Jews were first accused of ritual murder, and the coronation of Richard I in 1189 marked the
beginning, here too, of a period of massacres and royal exactions in the name of protection. The end was the expulsion of the Jews in 1290. From then on until 1656 there
were virtually no Jews in England. Then the Puritans, in
line with their reinstatement of the Old Testament, opened
the country to Jewish marranos from Spain, Portugal and
Holland, availed themselves of their commercial and diplomatic skill in British trade ventures, colonial expeditions

and wars with Holland, Spain and Portugal, and even appointed them to high office.

On the other side of Europe, the persecutions in Germany drove many Jews into Austria, Hungary and the Slav countries. What had happened to the Jews in the south and west of Europe, now happened to them in the east, only much faster.

Austria, Bohemia and Hungary, to be sure, had long had their Jews, who had come as traders in the wake of colonization from the West, and also from the Roman and Byzantine Balkans in the South. The Prague community is very ancient, and in Hungary there is indeed evidence of Jewish settlements even in Roman times, before the occupation by the Magyars. But it was only after the Crusades, with the inflow of fugitives from Germany, that the Jewish communities of these countries rose to high importance. The Bohemian Jews did not escape the ravages of the crusading gangs and many of them fled to Hungary and Poland. But later, under the reign of King Ottokar II in Bohemia, under the Dukes of Babenberg in Austria and the Arpad rulers in Hungary, the Jews enjoyed not only lasting protection, equality of rights, self-government and liberty of domicile, but even special prerogatives because, as everywhere else, they were needed for the development of trade and the money economy. In Hungary at that time Jews, Christians, Mohammedans and pagans lived together in untroubled concord. The repeated attempts of the Church and the popes to foster suppression of the Jews had no durable success. The Hungarian King Koloman (1096-1116) indeed treated the crusading hordes, which made their appearance in his country too, as robbers and accordingly just killed them. This is why the Hungarians were long decried as "pagans" or "Jews" in Western Europe. Both in Austria and in Hungary Jews were the rulers' financial advisers and even "Count Chamberlains" (*Kammergrafen*), mint-masters, administrators of princely estates and themselves also landowners, for here the feudal system did not develop until the thirteenth century. One of these Jewish counts, Teckanus, still owned extensive estates in Austria and Hungary at the beginning of the thirteenth century, as well as a palatial·mansion in Vienna. But toward the end of the Middle Ages, in Austria and Bohemia from the fourteenth century and in Hungary only from the sixteenth century onward, the Jews were overtaken by the same destiny as had befallen them in Western Europe.

In Hungary, and even more so in Poland, the flow of Jewish immigrants from the West linked up with another from the East, which originated on the northern shores of the Black Sea, in the Crimea and the Caucasus. Many Jews had fled there in the eighth and ninth centuries from the Byzantine persecutions, and simultaneously the Arab expansion in Asia Minor had driven to the same regions the Khazars, a Turkish tribe. These latter founded a powerful empire on both sides of the Volga estuary, from the Caucasus to the Urals, and gradually ousted the Byzantines from the Crimea. This tribe was a unique phenomenon in world history, insofar as, being wooed by three religions, Christianity, Islam and Judaism, it chose Judaism. Letters that have come down to us from the tenth century relate how the Khazar king summoned representatives of the three religions to a disputation, the result of which was his conversion to Judaism. This story was developed philosophically by Judah Halevi, the great Hebrew poet of Spain, in his book *Kuzari*. For two centuries the Khazars, who intermarried widely with the Jews, ruled the lands on the Caspian and Black Sea as far as the Slavs on the southern Dnieper, and their far-flung trade reached up to Sweden. But then a similar religious disputation won over to Byzantium Vladimir I, prince of all Russia (980-1015), who adopted the Byzantine creed; between them the two soon made an end to the "Jewish Empire." Parts of the Khazar tribe thereupon joined with Byzantine Jews in founding the Jewish settlements in eastern countries, in Kievan Russia, in Rumania and Poland. Some of them were swept into Hungary by the Magyar invasion.

However, like other eastern countries, Poland developed into a great center of Jewry only after the inflow of fugitive Jews in consequence of the Crusades and numerous later persecutions in the West. Together with the Jews, many Germans arrived, themselves fugitives from the civil wars during the German interregnum in the second half of the thirteenth century. Poland at that time was still an exclusively agricultural country, consisting only of landlords and peasants. Jewish and German immigrants first laid the foundations for the rise of the cities, first introduced trade and the money economy. Side by side, German and autonomous Jewish communities arose, whose members enjoyed liberty of domicile and trade, and protection from the hostility of the Church. Indeed, the self-governing community (*Kahal*) here attained to quite extraordinary power and administrative development, which originated in its overall fiscal responsibility to the king and gradually turned inward to become almost a state within a state. The town council was a complete, elected Jewish government. Several such *Kahals* would often join together in district or county associations, which met in regular diets (*Vaadim*) to discuss all the legal, administrative and cultural affairs of Jewry, to distribute taxation equitably and to act as the political representatives of the Jews vis-à-vis the king.

In its turn, this statelike organization of the Polish communities is the explanation of another characteristic feature of Polish Jewry, namely, its comprehensive and unitary school system. All boys between the ages of six and thirteen were obliged to attend elementary school (*Cheder*), where they learnt reading, writing and arithmetic, and were taught the Bible in the original text together with some of the easier Talmud treatises and commentaries. There were

private schools for the more well-to-do, and free community schools for the children of the poor and for orphans.
But all schools were under the control of the community.
For higher studies, each urban community had a higher
Talmud school (*Jeshivah*), whose "rector" was the rabbi
and whose students were maintained at the expense of the
community, so that, free from the cares of earning a livelihood, they should devote themselves exclusively to learning.
While this is evidence of the communities' high esteem and
respect for erudition, it also had practical implications for
their self-government. Jewish law was still everywhere religious law, it was derived from the Talmud and interpreted
on its basis and on that of the vast literature of its commentators; the juridical parts of the Talmud itself were an
interpretation of biblical law. The more autonomous the
Jewish communities were and the more the Jews lived apart
from their Christian surroundings within their own legal
order, the more they concentrated their studies on the
Halakha, the legal code of the Talmud. Thus the Talmud
schools were essentially schools of religious law. And since,
now as in ancient times, religious law governed the entire
life of pious Jews, the famous rabbis and heads of schools
had binding authority over the people. Rather as in Christian scholasticism, the rivalry between different schools
gradually degenerated into a struggle for victory in debate,
and into that extreme, hair-splitting casuistry which, as *"pil-
pul"* (meaning pepper) later wrongly came to be regarded
as the essence of Talmudism in general. Contemporary Jewish scholars in the West complained even then that the living significance of the questions and the sources was being
buried under the *l'art pour l'art* of dialectical fencing.
Ultimately, of course, Polish Talmudism reacted back upon
Central European Jewry.

While in the West the Jews had since the twelfth century
been restricted to the sole trade of moneylending, in the
East they were merchants, especially salt and spice mer-

chants, and traded on a large scale as far as the Black Sea, Constantinople, Genoa and Venice. Furthermore, they farmed royal excises and state taxes, and the usufruct of mines and forests. Here too, in time, Christian competition and the customary persecutions squeezed the Jews out of independent farming and, at least in part, of merchandise trade. But, unlike what had happened in Western Europe, they were left with two other ways of earning a living besides moneylending, namely, crafts and tenant farming.

The Jews exercised their crafts under royal privileges, they formed guilds of their own (as, incidentally, did Spanish Jews in the thirteenth and fourteenth centuries) which, like the Christian guilds, had a religious character, and entered into agreements with their Christian counterparts about how to share out the custom. Against payment of certain fees Jewish artisans could even acquire the right to keep Christian apprentices, as well as a seat in the guild court and other privileges. The Jews had almost a monopoly as pewterers and coppersmiths, and similarly they far outnumbered their Christian colleagues as tailors, glaziers, furriers, bookbinders and in other trades. In Poland, as also in Bohemia, there were, incidentally, a good many Jewish musicians.

But the other main occupation with which the Jews ended up, tenant farming, forced them into as hateful a role as moneylending had in Western Europe. The power of the Polish kings, who nearly always favored the Jews, was being undermined by the oligarchy of the aristocratic landowners, and up and down the countryside the Jews fell under the sway of the local squires on whose estates they lived. These squires preferred to live in the big cities and to devote themselves to politics and their pleasures; they used Jewish tenants to administer their estates for them, and by asking exorbitant rents, forced them to squeeze and grind the peasants. Like the farming of alehouses, which similarly became the business of Jews, this was not only in itself a degrading occupation, but it also roused against the Jews the hatred of the common people, who lost no opportunity of giving vent to their rancor in pogroms and persecution of all kinds. The Jews' masters never dreamt of protecting them. Furthermore, as time went on, sheer business envy, together with the influence of the Church in the towns and diets and with the kings, gradually led to the same debasement and forcible segregation of the Jews which already were the rule everywhere else in Europe.

To begin with, the Jews were confined in ghettos, or else they were assigned small towns as their exclusive residence, such as, for instance, Kasimierz near Cracow; later they were chased out of the towns into the countryside and the villages.

Finally, around the middle of the seventeenth century, a catastrophe comparable to the Crusades occurred in the western parts of the Slav lands. The Ukrainian cossacks and peasants, who were cruelly oppressed by the Polish nobility, rose in a mighty insurrection and, led by an impoverished nobleman, Chmielnicky, they devastated the villages and towns of eastern Galicia (Red Russia), White Russia and Lithuania. Betrayed by the nobles and the townsmen, whom they had helped in their fight, any Jews who did not manage to escape were slain. Soon the Russian armies invaded Poland from the East and the Swedes broke in from the North—and all alike savaged the Jews. More than seven hundred communities were destroyed or cruelly decimated; barely one tenth of the Jewish population of the Polish Ukraine, of Volhynia and Podolia survived the catastrophe. Streams of fugitives set off in the opposite direction, back to where they had come from, to the countries of Central and Western Europe. These countries were not, at the time, so thoroughly and rigidly organized that, despite all the restrictions, expulsions and persecutions, Jews could not find a refuge there, especially since the

Western Jews welcomed the refugees with open arms everywhere.

The Ukrainian revolt was to repeat itself later, upon the instigation of the Orthodox Church in its struggle against the Catholic Church. Grotesquely, the Jews then shed their blood not only for the Poles, but for Catholicism to boot. For Polish Jewry these revolts were what the Crusades had been for German Jewry: there was no recovery. The *Kahal* fell into poverty and decay, and lost its authority and political role; its associations crumbled away, its diets ceased. The schools lay deserted, bereft of the famed scholars who had fled westward, especially to Italy and Holland. For better or for worse, most Jews were at the mercy of the Polish nobility.

The utter hopelessness of the Jewish position fostered the emergence of messianic and mystic currents. From their obscure depths there rose once more a wonderful flowering of the spirit. It came in the eighteenth century, one of the finest, wisest and tenderest movements in human history, comparable to early Christianity: the Hasidic school of Ba'al Shem Tobh. Its doctrine of pure service to humanity, of inward lay piety and humble joy of life was diametrically opposed to the Talmudic scholasticism and ritualism. Hasidism is the finest flower of the Jewish way of life as it developed in the Middle Ages: the complete isolation of Jewish existence from its environment and the flow of history, its enclosure in an archaic world which had become an inner dream world. To be sure, it also reflected the specific circumstances of the Slav areas—rural circumstances, for there the Jews lived in villages and small towns and not only in the airless, stuffy lanes of the ghetto. Hence Hasidism smiles at nature, reflects the mood of a gentle flocking together for warmth and comfort in the face of the mighty, potentially ever-explosive pressure from outside; it reflects the small pleasures of life, intimate customs, the family, and also the extravagant, fantastic hopes of the Messiah. The primordial past is inextricably interwoven with a utopian future; the figures of the patriarchs, of the whole of biblical history, are as close and alive as fathers and brothers, their destinies are told and talked over like family reminiscences. And just as close and present is the Messiah, who enters at any moment or may enter, and are the demons, exorcised by the pure spirit of the pious.

After the partitions of Poland in the eighteenth and nineteenth centuries most of the Polish Jews found themselves living in Russia. In the Polish national rising under Kosciuszko the Jews had fought in a volunteer legion, whose leader afterward, under Napoleon, fell for Polish independence. But now the destinies of the Polish and Lithuanian Jews were united with those of the Russian ones, and once more Jewry had new prospects and the task of economic pioneering work in the vast spaces of this economically still dormant empire.

The history of the Jews in Russia had so far been one of separate episodes. Quite early, Jewish traders had come from Byzantium and the Khazar Empire to the banks of the Volga and the Dnieper. And when their Khazar empire crumbled and the Khazars fled to the principality of Kiev, Jews went along with them and founded communities which soon got into lively religious rivalry with Byzantine Christianity. Jews played an important part in the trade which passed through the Slav countries on its way from Western Europe to the Orient. But this trade was interrupted by the Mongol invasion in the thirteenth century, and until the end of the fifteenth century Jews hardly ever reached the Muscovite realm. At that time, Jews from Kiev, Lithuania and Western Europe met again at Novgorod, the great northern emporium, where Christianity was still as unstable as it had been in Western Europe before the turn of the millennium; soon the Jews became the nucleus of a group of Judaizers, nobles and even Church dignitaries, who repudiated the divine nature of Christ, the Trinity and the cult of images. The movement penetrated as far as Moscow, to the court of the Czar. The furious counterattack of the Orthodox Church had the result that Russia long remained closed to the Jews; only a few privileged merchants from Poland and Lithuania were allowed entry. From then onward until the mid-nineteenth century all czarist governments adopted the same characteristic policy toward the Jews: they confined them within the so-called Pale of Settlement, that is, permitted them to live only in specified areas of the country.

Once, when the Polish king interceded in favor of his Jewish merchants, the then Czar Ivan the Terrible (1533-1584) declared that he would not allow the Jews into Moscow because they alienated the Russians from their faith and brought poisonous weeds (namely, tobacco) into the country. There were no bounds to the range of suspicions which were cast upon the Jews; a characteristic example is the rumor spread by the first Romanov czars, to the effect that the "false Dimitri," who for a short while usurped the czarist throne (1605-1608), had been a Jew. The policy of keeping the Jews out remained unchanged, at least so far as the interior of the country was concerned; they were allowed only into the frontier areas, when they came as traveling merchants. Even the enlightened Peter the Great was no exception, although he favored marranos and the baptized descendants of Jews and indeed protected the native Jews against the attacks of the clergy and the accusations of ritual murder; his ambassadors in Vienna and London were of Jewish origin. But the czarinas Catherine I and Elizabeth eventually began to expel from Russia even the native Jews who refused conversion to the Orthodox Church, though for economic reasons the expulsions could not be put into practice. Contrary to what happened in the economically advanced countries of Western Europe, an attempt was made in Russia to restrict the Jews to wholesale trade and to drive them out of the markets and fairs. But that, too, proved impossible. For the sake of trade development, the Czarina Catherine II (1762-1892) ultimately had to allow Jews to settle in the thinly populated southern region of the Empire.

The partition of Poland brought 200,000 Jews under Russian rule, and this sudden and large-scale influx turned the integration of the Jews into a chronic problem insoluble in the given, contradictory circumstances. On the one hand, it remained official policy to segregate the Jews and to domicile them in specific, exclusive territories, even to the point of reviving the institution of the *Kahal*. On the other hand, the influence of the Enlightenment led to forcible attempts to Christianize and Russify the Jews. In neither case could there be any real hope of success. Segregation was disrupted by a rising class of businessmen who knew how to take advantage of the new opportunities for large-scale commercial and later industrial enterprise and whom the economy simply could not spare—nor, for that matter, could the army, for which they became indispensable purveyors. In its turn, assimilation foundered on the Jews' unwillingness to give up their religion and on the impossibility of getting them quickly, and by such methods, out of the cultural enclave into which centuries of isolation and material oppression had driven them. There was the added difficulty of the Christian population's animosity and hostility, which were ceaselessly fanned by the implacable instigations of the Orthodox Church and kept alert by the capricious and arbitrary attitude of successive czarist governments, which again and again succumbed to reactionary tendencies.

By and large, therefore, nothing much changed, or rather, change was very slow. The Jewish masses remained poor; they were still small tenants, artisans or publicans, even though the attempt was made, with quite inadequate means and abuses of authority, either to dislodge the Jews from the countryside and drive them into the towns, or else to settle them in distant agricultural colonies. When compulsory military service was introduced in 1827, the Jews were made to contribute a higher proportion of conscripts than the rest of the population, were made to serve a twenty-five-year term and altogether were treated even worse and left with even fewer rights than the general run of soldiers in the czarist armies. With the beginning of industrialization, many Jews flocked into the factories and, especially in Poland, came to account for a sizeable part of the industrial labor force. All this did at least something to pry them loose from their old way of life. But real improvement was limited to the Jewish capitalists and intellectuals, who began to assimilate when the schools were opened to Jews; in their case the barriers did fall, at least partly and superficially. But pogroms and accusations of ritual murder occurred as late as the twentieth century. In these parts the Middle Ages in fact lasted until the Russian revolution in 1917.

In Western and Central Europe, meanwhile, the persecution of Jews continued, after the Crusades, well into the early centuries of the modern age. Again and again superstition and religious fanaticism erupted here and there into large-scale massacres, not to mention smaller, local excesses. In southern Germany around the year 1300, upon a rumor that Jews had profaned the host, the Frankish knight Rindfleisch set forth on an expedition of murder and plunder which claimed 140 Jewish communities and more than 100,000 individuals as its victims; in France in 1320, the erroneous report of a new crusade set off an uprising of shepherds (*pastoureaux*), which destroyed 120 communities; between 1336 and 1338 "Jew-baiter" or "arm-leather" gangs (so called because they wore a leather band on their arms for identification) made devastating attacks on Jews in Alsatia, the Rhineland, Swabia and Austria; in 1349 there followed persecutions by the flagellants, bands of

frenzied ascetics, at the time when the Black Death was
spreading to Europe and the Jews were accused of having
caused it by poisoning wells; in 1422 the Jews suffered, as
in all persecutions of heretics, under the struggle against
the Hussite reformation; and from 1481 onward they were
burnt in the Inquisition. All this is recorded in the Jewish
chronicles and martyrologies.

The Reformation, with its return to the original text of
the Bible and appreciation of the Old Testament, might
have been expected to lead to a change of attitude toward
the Jews, the more so as they had had to suffer cruelly
under the violent reaction of Catholicism against all reform
movements. And indeed, in an early tract *That Jesus Christ
Was Born a Jew,* Luther in 1523 sharply censured the
Church for its persecution of the Jews: "The fools, popes,
bishops, sophists and monks, these rough blockheads, have
until now so dealt with the Jews that any good Christian
would have preferred to be a Jew. . . . Like dogs they treated
the Jews, abused them and took away what was theirs. . . .
And yet they are kinsmen, cousins and brothers of our
Lord. . . . But if we always drive them with an iron hand,
accuse them of needing Christian blood so as not to smell
foul, and all other manner of folly . . . what good can we
do them that way? Likewise, if we forbid them to exercise
their trade among us and keep other human contacts,
which drives them into usury, how is that to improve them?
To help them, one must apply to them the law of Christian, not of popish love, welcome them kindly and allow
them to work and earn their living, so that they may get
to know from their own experience the doctrine and life
of Christians." But it soon turned out that even Luther saw
kindness and justice toward the Jews as merely another,
and more effective, method to the same end, namely, their
conversion. And when this result failed to come about as
quickly as he had expected, Luther—like Mohammed before him, who had initially wooed the Jews—turned his full

fury against this "stubborn people." The only ones to defend the Jews for the sake of justice and tolerance alone at that time were those precursors of the Enlightenment, the humanists, and especially the valorous Reuchlin.

In time, as the political order of Europe was consolidated, massacres became less frequent. The last persecution in the grand style was a concomitant of the chaotic conditions and religious fanaticism of the Thirty Years' War. Expulsions, on the other hand, continued regularly until the mid-eighteenth century, the last instance occurring in 1744, when the Empress Maria Theresa temporarily banned the Jews from Prague. Jews were expelled from cities and districts far too often to be recorded here. The first country to evict them entirely from the whole of its territory was England, in 1290. At that time the Jews fled to the neighboring countries on the west coast of the European continent. But a century later, in 1394, they were expelled from France and wandered on into Flanders and Brabant in Belgium, into Savoy, Germany, Spain and Italy. The only place in France where they managed to hang on was in the southern dependencies, in Provence, especially in the ports where their economic position was too firmly established and important, and also in the papal territories of Avignon and Carpentras; even there, however, they were frequently tossed hither and thither by the changing favor and disfavor of local circumstances and, driven out of one place, would find refuge in another.

Yet another century later, in 1492, the Jews were driven out of Spain. This event marked a further landslide in the destinies of European Jewry. Until then, Spain, among all the countries of Europe, had been the land where Jews were most numerous and also, next to Poland, socially and culturally in the highest position and most actively involved in national development. With the advance of Christian against Moorish Spain in the thirteenth century, the center of gravity of Spanish Jewry had shifted from the Moslem to the Christian areas, to Castile and Aragon. The Christian sovereigns of these countries had learnt from the Moslem ones to value and use the services and abilities of the Jews. They continued to employ them as treasurers, physicians and diplomats, as tax farmers and army purveyors, and, like the aristocracy in its castles, personally frequented Jewish scholars and poets. Jews financed their military ventures, Jewish astronomers paved the way for their voyages of discovery overseas. The Portuguese Prince Henry the Navigator (1394-1460) founded a school of navigation and appointed as its head Jahuda Cresques (Jaime of Mallorca), the foremost expert at the time in cartography, navigation and nautical instruments, which latter he made himself. It is now an established historical fact that Jews had a major part in the expeditions of Columbus, which they promoted, financed and actively participated in; Columbus' Jewish interpreter, the linguist Luis de Torres, was the first European on these expeditions to step upon American soil. There is indeed a strong presumption that Columbus himself was a Jewish marrano. Just as they were to have later in Poland, the Jews in Spain had powerful autonomous communities, whose constitution rivaled that of Christian cities. As in Poland, Jewish craftsmen were organized in guilds. Some small communities consisted almost exclusively of artisans, especially smiths and masons. But all other trades were open to the Jews, who excelled especially as wool weavers, piece-goods merchants, overseas traders and in finance.

This situation, however, was untenable in a Europe in which the tide of hatred against the Jews was rising everywhere, in which the Inquisition spread its tentacles, and in which Christian business competition found so convenient a weapon in the arguments of the Church; what is more, Spain was an outpost of Christianity and as such the country where the religious passions kindled by the war against the infidels had survived longest. The beginning of the

end came with the large-scale persecutions in the fourteenth century, with the destruction of the prosperous Jewish communities and the abrogation of Jewish rights in
Aragon. The Jews retreated into Castile, the last bulwark
of their liberty. Isabella and Ferdinand, who, from 1474
onward, ruled over a united Castile and Aragon, had continued to fortify their power and to finance their liberation
campaign against the Moors with Jewish money, furnished
to them by Don Abraham Senior in his capacity both as
banker and as general tax collector. But soon a sort of
religious race theory developed under the influence of the
Church; true Spanish blood was to prove itself by the special vigor of its Christian faith. After the conquest of
Granada (1492) and the elimination of the last vestiges of
Islamic rule from the whole peninsula, the Spanish sovereigns undertook the internal nationalization of their country. This step signified Christian purification, and Moors
and Jews were expelled. The Jews divided up into three
groups. One group openly held fast to its religion and
chose martyrdom by fire or emigration; the second went
underground, as we would say today, by publicly accept-
ing Christianity but secretly remaining Jews—which did not
prevent their having to leave the country later, under
pressure from the Inquisition; and lastly a third group intermingled with the Christian population and lost its identity
in it. By the middle of the sixteenth century the process of
assimilation was all but complete. But when, in 1580, the
Habsburg King Philip II united Spain and Portugal, the
whole of Spain was flooded by Portuguese marranos, who
were called "merchants of Hebrew or Portuguese origin,"
or simply Jews, and they gradually assumed the heritage
of exiled Jews in medicine, jurisprudence and the economy.

The Spanish expulsion had significant repercussions in
the most divers parts of Europe. Marranos emigrated to
southern France, especially to Bordeaux, Bayonne and Tou-
louse, and there quickly rose to great prosperity. The later

French kings, especially Louis XIV, showed them much favor because of their economic ability. When, during the first half of the eighteenth century, these people once more openly confessed themselves Jews, they thus replenished the Jewish population of France, together with the Jews of Lorraine and Alsace who came under French rule with the incorporation of these provinces. There was long a sharp division between the two main branches of the tree of French Jewry—the Spanish-Portuguese Sephardim and the Ashkenazim from Alsace-Lorraine, the former with their past Spanish glory feeling themselves to be as superior to the latter as the enlightened and assimilated German Jews were later to feel to the Eastern Jews still stuck in their orthodoxy.

Spanish emigrants also went to Italy, where government measures were never taken seriously, and where, in any event, the multiple rulers and changes thereof always provided a haven in an emergency. Fleeing still farther east, Spanish Jews also went to the Balkans, where in 1453 the Turks had conquered Constantinople.

In Turkey, they were able to live on in the traditions of their great past. Here, after the persecutions in Christian lands, they experienced a peaceful respite, freedom from all discriminatory measures, and they found the lasting favor of the sultans, who chose them for their ministers, physicians and expert advisers. Sultan Bayezid II (1481-1512) is reported once to have said with surprise, speaking of the Spanish immigrants: "You call Fernando a wise king—he, who has impoverished his country and enriched ours!" And in fact the Jewish communities in Constantinople, at Adrianople and Brusa, and the one at Salonica, which the Sephardim revived and which was to be destroyed by the Nazis, were the leaders in a new era of social and intellectual prosperity. In the sixteenth century Turkey was the great Kabbala center and the birthplace of a number of prophetic and messianic movements. It was in

Turkey, too, that Joseph Karo wrote his *Shulhan Arukh,* the most representative modern encyclopedia of Talmudic law and ritual. The Portuguese marrano Joseph Nasi, who emigrated to Turkey in 1553 and at once openly reverted to Judaism, became a powerful statesman of the Turkish Empire and as such was much courted by European princes and ministers. He conquered Cyprus for the Sultan, who made him Duke of Naxos. He was also a patron of Jewish scholars, promoted Jewish schools in Constantinople, and founded a special printing press for Hebrew literature. When Pope Paul IV was threatening the Jews in the papal territory of Ancona, Nasi saved them by a trade boycott of the papal port. With the subsequent decline of the Turkish Empire, Turkish Jewry, too, declined. Here, too, the country's own Orthodox Christians and Jesuits eventually raised the blood-guilt charge against the Jews and incited the people to hatred against them. Therefore in the eighteenth century many Turkish Jews moved to Vienna, where they had special privileges under Ottoman protection and founded a Turkish colony.

But the most important consequences of the Spanish policy of Catholic national purification manifested themselves at the opposite end of the European continent, namely, in the Low Countries, which, as a consequence of intermarriage between the Burgundian and Habsburg dynasties, had been brought under Spanish rule. During the second half of the sixteenth century the Protestant parts of these provinces fought and won the battle for their independence and set themselves up as a free republic. In the Catholic part, which remained with Spain and is now Belgium, Jews had been living as early as the fourth century, when Belgium was still an outpost of Gaul, as it later was of France. Subsequently the country fell to Burgundy, and French Jews fled there after expulsion from France at the end of the fourteenth century. In Holland, on the other hand, Jewish settlement did not really begin until the immigration

of Spanish and Portuguese marranos into the Netherlands
Republic at the end of the sixteenth century. This late
settlement quickly became one of the most important of
modern European Jewry, and its influences and ramifications extended into other European countries. The marrano
immigrants, who at once confessed their Judaism, were
subject to considerable social and economic restrictions,
but, since most of them had arrived well provided with
capital, they soon moved into leading economic positions
in the young republic and advanced its economic development. The Jewish colony at Amsterdam did much to turn
the city into a center of world trade and to raise it above
its rival, Antwerp. Once more the Jews made themselves
especially useful by virtue of their far-flung international
connections, their link with the marranos in the Orient and
their old tradition in world trade. The Jews founded large
merchant shipping and banking firms. There were Jews
among the financiers and directors of the West India and
East India companies, which were the pioneers of Dutch
colonial power. The Jews showed their gratitude to the
Netherlands state for not treating them as mere objects and
instruments of exploitation, as European rulers had done
so far; they backed the state's political ventures with huge
sums and fought in its wars. According to the Dutch historian, Van Hogendorf, the Jewish banker de Pinto saved
the state in the war with France. The prominent Jewish
families of Pinto, d'Acosta, Texeira and others, lived in
great style in magnificent palaces and country houses; the
Sephardic synagogue of Amsterdam was a famous eighteenth century building. From Germany and especially
from the Slav countries, after the catastrophe which befell
the Polish and Lithuanian Jews, there eventually came a
stream of Ashkenazic families who founded their own communities in Holland. They specialized in diamond cutting,
a typically Jewish skill originally introduced by the Se-

phardim, which was later to become almost a Jewish monopoly in the trade in precious stones in Holland.

Here, as everywhere else where life was kind to the Jews, their intellectual forces throve and they produced famous physicians, scholars of encyclopedic learning and worldwide reputation, writers, and patrons of the arts. Rembrandt's paintings testify to their social and cultural significance, and distinguished Jews were among his personal friends. This was the atmosphere in which Spinoza grew up, and it was no accident that with him for the first time since the Spanish Middle Ages, Jewish thought broke through its own religious barriers and once more gained universal influence. To be sure, the Dutch communities distinguished themselves by a specifically religious discipline, which they had brought from Spain where Catholic fanaticism and the dangers of marranism had forced the Jews in their turn into extreme Orthodoxy. But on the other hand, Holland was the first great seat of Enlightenment, where freethinkers from all over the world could print the works which they were unable to publish at home. The new ideas gained ground among the higher social and intellectual strata of the Jews, who always and everywhere were among the intellectual avant-garde. And thus Holland became the scene of the first breakthrough of free thought in its struggle against Orthodoxy, which led to the famous episode of the religious excommunication of Spinoza and Uriel d'Acosta. Spinoza's philosophy marks the transition from Jewish Orthodoxy and Jewish mysticism to secular, rationalistic thought, just as in the old days Philo of Alexandria and Moses Maimonides had established a link between Jewish and Greek thought.

The rise of Dutch Jewry bore fruit elsewhere. The tale of the benefits which Jewish immigration had brought the young republic spread to northern countries, and in 1622 the King of Denmark invited Dutch Jews to settle at Glückstadt, a city of Holstein which he planned to develop into a great emporium and rival of Hamburg. In 1657, after the costly war with Sweden, additional Dutch Sephardic Jews were invited to settle in Denmark itself, thus laying the foundation for the Copenhagen community. In Sweden, the first permanent Jewish settlement did not appear until the end of the eighteenth century, and in Norway even later, around the mid-nineteenth century. In both cases the Jewish settlements were originally mostly ramifications of the great community in the Hansa city of Hamburg, which community had been founded in the sixteenth century by Portuguese refugees. Today's Norwegian name Hambro owes its origin to this Hamburg association. (Carl Joachim Hambro was president of the Storting, and Norwegian representative at the League of Nations.)

Finally, the Dutch influence was instrumental in accomplishing the readmittance of Jews to England. The first breach there had meanwhile been made by the immigration of the Portuguese marrano Antonio Fernandez Carvajal, who arrived in London around 1635 as a powerful merchant and, as soon as his position was firmly established, had avowed his Judaism. His merchant ships plied the oceans to the East and West Indies, to Brazil and the Levant, and he had agencies in all the great European centers of commerce. Gradually a whole group of rich and cultivated marranos collected around him; they took part as advisers and financiers in Britain's colonial ventures and some of them occupied official positions. But the question of right of domicile was raised only later by the Dutch rabbi and scholar Manasseh ben Israel, a world famous seventeenth-century theologian and friend and correspondent of Hugo Grotius, Rembrandt and Queen Christina of Sweden. Manasseh ben Israel had fallen under the sway of the time's mystical and messianic currents in Judaism; he believed in the messianic promise that, once the Jews were dispersed over the whole earth, the Redeemer would

come and lead them back to their homeland in Palestine.
To promote this dispersal of the Jews, he addressed to the
English Council of State and Parliament in 1650 a remark-
able treatise, *Esperança de Israel* (the Hope of Israel), and
later to Cromwell an outright petition for the return of
the Jews to the British Isles. Although no general right of
domicile was conceded to the Jews, many individuals were
from then on again allowed to settle in England. Among
others, German Jews immigrated, and refugees from Poland
after the Chmielnicky massacres. How vital Jewish capital
became for England is shown by the case of the banker
Sampson Gideon, who, in 1745, raised no less than 1.7 million pounds for the then hard-pressed government and
eventually staked his own fortune to save the country from
bankruptcy. After Gideon there has been an uninterrupted
line of English Jewish bankers, from the Salvadors to the
Rothschilds.

In 1723 Jews born in England obtained the right to own
land. But when the fight for equal rights again and again
encountered new obstacles, some of the successful Jewish
families accepted baptism and, like many before them in
Spain, melted into the native aristocracy. Others persevered
until the full emancipation of the Jews, which was achieved
step by step in the course of the nineteenth century.

Gradually the Enlightenment loosened the degrading and
intolerable restrictions which since the Crusades had cut
off the Jews from life and air. The Enlightenment weakened the power of the Churches and religious prejudices, it
proclaimed the equality and natural rights of all men,
taught that the world was governed by physical laws, demanded dispassionate, rational inquiry into facts, and
preached tolerance and humanity. At first, in this era, it all
amounted merely to a growing general mood which to
some extent favored the Jewish aspirations to escape from
the ghettos. And only a few privileged Jews gained a sem-

blance of equality with other people, and they did so by one means only: money. Jews had to concentrate upon money, for it was their only protection, their only road to freedom. Whenever Jews were free, before then or after, money was never more for them than one aim among many others and played no dominating part. But in the age of the ghetto their environment forced them above all into the pursuit of gain.

We have seen how the Jews, especially in Central Europe, had gradually been excluded from all occupations until they were confined to small-scale money trading— moneylending, pawnbroking and moneychanging. They sought in every way to broaden their sphere of activity, and this was necessarily against the law. Pawnbroking developed into trade with unredeemed pledges—peddling and second-hand trade. This latter in turn branched out into trade in all kinds of new merchandise acquired by stealth and in circumvention of the already disintegrating guilds. This was the origin of two branches of business in which Jews later traditionally excelled: general stores and the garment trade. Trade in clothes led, very early, in Frankfurt-am-Main, to the manufacture of ready-made clothes. Pawnbroking in its turn was the origin of the Jewish trade in gold and precious stones. Finally, it was their mixed merchandise trade that suited the Jews especially well, for the important role it fulfilled in the supplying of military resources; a Danish corps in the seventeenth century, for example, is reported to have had no fewer than seven hundred Jewish purveyors and victualers.

These were the ways by which individual Jews gradually acquired considerable prosperity. A number of different circumstances helped them on. Jewish merchants from the East used to travel to German markets and trade fairs to buy on behalf of Poland, Russia and Turkey. On these occasions native Jews served as intermediaries and business associates, which gave them a fair profit. Those who had already accumulated capital of some size, saw new and larger opportunities open up to them. The Holy Roman Empire of the Habsburgs was, at that time, disintegrating into a number of larger and smaller territorial states, whose rulers broke away from the suzerainty of the Emperor and the influence of the Estates, and set up an absolute rule on the model of the French kings. This required the maintenance of a sumptuous, representative court and of armies for the perennial power struggle; and that in turn required more money than ever. For this reason the princes were anxious to raise their tax revenues by promoting trade and industry, and to collect them more effectively by stricter administration. But the regular revenues never sufficed, so that in addition finance credits were needed. Just at that time the shift of world trade from the Mediterranean to the Atlantic coasts, which came in the wake of the opening up of America, had ruined or at least greatly weakened the great German capitalists of the Renaissance, such as the Fuggers, Welsers and Tuchers. Their place was now taken by the Jews who, in the manner described, had accumulated some wealth. They became the financiers of the princes —not so much like the gentile Renaissance bankers, as independent lenders, for they were not as yet rich enough to supply the necessary sums from their own funds, but rather as employees, as financial agents. They arranged loans at the big trading centers of the West. In addition they farmed and administered taxes, the mint, the Crown mines, forests and salines, granted loans on the state demesne or indeed on the treasure of the Crown and the sovereign's jewels, and acted as army purveyors on a large scale. A man who thus combined all these multiple functions in his own person was called a court factor, and in the seventeenth and eighteenth centuries almost all princes in Germany and Central Europe had their own Jewish court factors. These men often gained much power and influence and, by virtue of their international connections and the growing importance of trade and finance, often came to play a major part in politics as well. There was hardly any sizeable military operation at that time that was not launched with the support of Jewish bankers. In Vienna, Samuel Oppenheimer was "Imperial Chief Military Factor"; nearly all the large supply contracts for food and munitions were negotiated through him. His business associate, Diego Texeira d'Aguilar, a Portuguese marrano, organized the Tobacco Administration not only in Portugal but also in Austria. Some of these Jewish bankers, like the Arnsteins, Wertheimers and Eskeles', were raised to the nobility; the first of them was Jakob Bassevi von Treuenberg of Prague, in 1622. The court of Berlin employed Jewish bankers and treasurers as early as the sixteenth century. Even bishops availed themselves of their services, and so did the Teutonic Order. Not only native Jews were involved, for often it was the practice to turn to foreign banking firms or to employ financial agents from elsewhere. Between 1690 and 1790 Frankfurt-am-Main alone provided no fewer than thirty-three court factors for the most diverse princely houses. All in all, Frankfurt-am-Main at that time developed into the most important trading and financial center of Europe along with Amsterdam and Hamburg, thanks not least to the economic activity of Frankfurt Jews. The town was the cradle of many of the great international Jewish families of the eighteenth and nineteenth centuries, to mention only such names as Rothschild, Speyer, Fuld, Schiff, Stern, Weisweiler, Königswarter, etc. It was to Frankfurt that smaller and poorer countries turned to raise capital for their colonial and major private enterprises, and ultimately even to finance the construction of railways for the whole of North America. Thus the international position and ramification of the Jewish banking firms made a by no means negligible contribution to the development of capitalist economic techniques on a world scale.

As long as the Jewish financiers were in the fixed employ-

ment of princes and, on their behalf, had to squeeze every
last penny from the State's sources of revenue, they nat-
urally attracted the very special dislike of the population
and the envy of Christian officials. In addition, their position often involved them in political struggles, and more
than one of them had to pay for their power with their life;
examples are Lippold, the treasurer of the Elector of Bran-
denburg in the sixteenth century, and in the eighteenth
century the Württemberg finance minister and diplomat
Joseph Süss Oppenheimer (known as "Jew Süss," and a
member of the same Frankfurt family to which the above-
mentioned Vienna court factor belonged, the "Fugger of
his age"). Nevertheless, those great financiers and bankers
were the forerunners of the gradual emancipation and assimilation of the Jews. Thanks to special privileges they
became exempt from the general measures applicable to
Jews, and their growing number and importance, together
with the tolerant attitudes of the Age of Enlightenment, in
time led to a relaxation of those measures themselves. It
was becoming altogether too obvious how grotesque a contrast there was between the rising economic and cultural
prominence of the Jews and their disgraceful general subjugation.

Great Jewish bankers like Baron Arnstein and Baron
Eskeles in Vienna, and the Itzigs and Ephraims in Berlin,
entertained on a lavish scale and their brilliant salons were
the meeting places of high society—aristocrats, officers, diplomats and statesmen from all over the world, Talleyrand,
Mirabeau, Wellington, Hardenberg, as well as the avant-
garde of contemporary intellectuals. The literary salons of
Rahel Levin and Henriette Herz were the equivalent of
those of prerevolutionary Paris; they were the social head-
quarters of the "Berlin enlightenment" and the German
romantic movement. But at the same time the poor Jews
lived in crowded ghettos which it was prohibited to enlarge,
in "one long street," according to a traveler's description of

the Jewish district of Frankfurt in 1795, "closed in by five-
or six-story houses. Imagine these houses with their back
premises, and behind them perhaps yet further back premises, having yards barely big enough to admit daylight; all
nooks and crannies, right up to the roof, crammed with tiny
rooms teeming with thousands of people, who deem themselves lucky when they can get out of their caves and take
the air in the dirty and humid streets. . . . What space there
is in front of the houses is occupied all day long by men
and women going about the day's business, for in their
dwellings these miserable people could not possibly do any
work."

Jews were allowed into the Christian quarters only during the day, during business hours. On Sundays the gates of
the ghetto were not opened at all. When Jews traveled from
one city to another, they had to pay a "body tax," such as
was levied on cattle. In order to keep down the numbers
of the Jewish population, at about that time a really fiendish
marriage limitation was enacted; under Charles VI, only the
eldest son of any Jewish family was allowed to marry, and
even then there were further restrictions on the number of
progeny, which was either made to depend on the family's
wealth or subjected to exorbitant taxation. Special taxes
were in any case applied to whatever a Jew undertook and
whatever step he made. The "Ordinance for Jewry," promulgated in 1750 by Frederick (II) the Great of Prussia,
who, for all his liberalism and his exploitation of Jewish
capital was a fierce enemy of the Jews, was so harsh that
Mirabeau described it as *"une loi digne d'un cannibale."*
Moses Mendelssohn, one of the leading spirits of the philosophy of Enlightenment in Germany, a man of world
fame, the close friend of the German poet Lessing and the
model for the hero of the latter's drama *Nathan der Weise,*
had a permit of residence in Berlin only thanks to his job as
a bookkeeper in a factory. We have an eyewitness account
of the first meeting between Mendelssohn and Kant in 1777.

It happened in one of the lecture rooms of the University of Königsberg, and the scene is evidence not only of the whole paradoxical Jewish situation at the time, but also of the irrational cruelty of a mass bigotry which, once implanted in people's minds, automatically perpetuated itself for generation upon generation; by contrast, we also see in this scene the sudden flash of awareness of a humanity common to all.

"A small, misshapen Jew with a pointed beard and pronounced hunchback entered the lecture room without paying much attention to those present, but with timidly soft steps, and stopped not far from the entrance door. As usual derision and mockery broke out at once and eventually turned into finger-snapping, whistling and stamping; but to everyone's astonishment the stranger remained where he was as if transfixed, icily calm, and indeed to make it quite plain that he intended waiting for the Professor, pulled up an empty chair and sat down. People approached him, put questions to him, and he replied briefly and politely that he meant to stay in order to make Kant's acquaintance. Only the latter's appearance at last quieted the uproar. His lecture directed everyone's attention to other matters, and soon the audience was so carried away, so immersed in a flood of new ideas, that the Jew was long forgotten when, at the end of the lecture, he pushed through the crowd toward the cathedra with a violence strangely contrasting with his equanimity. Hardly had the students noticed him, when the mocking laughter broke out once more, only to give way at once to mute admiration, when Kant, having looked significantly at the stranger for a moment or two and heard the few words which the latter said, shook him warmly by the hand and then embraced him. Like wildfire the news went through the crowd: 'Moses

Mendelssohn! It is the Jewish philosopher from Berlin!,'
and the students respectfully stood aside to form a passage when the two philosophers, hand in hand, left the
lecture room." *

The struggle for Jewish emancipation began with sallies by
Christian scholars and writers. The first of these sallies was
John Toland's tract, *Reasons for Naturalizing the Jews in
Great Britain and Ireland on the Same Foot with all Other
Nations, Containing also a Defense of the Jews Against All
Vulgar Prejudices in All Countries* (London 1714). Next
came, in Germany, Lessing's drama *Nathan der Weise*
(1779) and in 1781 a pamphlet by Christian Wilhelm Dohm,
On the Civil Amelioration of the Condition of the Jews, in
which the condition of the Jews was laid bare to Christian
consciences. In France, the same ideas were upheld by
Mirabeau in a treatise on Moses Mendelssohn and the
political reform of the Jews, published in 1787. These two
latter works reflect the influence of the American Declaration of Independence, which, in 1776, was first in the Christian world to proclaim equality of rights for the Jews.

In Europe, there followed in 1782 the so-called *Toleranz-
patent* which the German Emperor Joseph II promulgated
for the Habsburg Empire under the impact of the American
Declaration of Independence and the generally spreading
tendencies of Enlightenment. This was the first European
attempt to liberate the Jews, but, like all the reforms of this
dilettante and doctrinaire Habsburg, it was anything but
tolerant. What he wanted was to carry through the assimilation of the Jews instantly and compulsorily, by decree, a
measure that had catastrophic consequences, especially in
the Orothodox communities of Galicia. The reforms were
soon abandoned under the reactionary reign of Joseph's successors. Jewish emancipation in Europe actually dates back

* H. Jolowicz, *Geschichte der Juden in Königsberg i Pr.* (Posen,
1867), p. 98.

to the French Revolution, when the Constituent Assembly in 1790 and 1791 granted the Jews full rights of citizenship. The armies of the revolution spread emancipation first to the neighboring countries, to Holland (1796) and Italy (1798) and the occupied German territories. Even Prussia granted the Jews citizenship during the brief burst of liberalism which accompanied the wars of liberation against Napoleon.

But all this was not to last. Already, in 1815, the Congress of Vienna repealed part of the new freedoms, and to establish them finally and fully required a long, tough struggle in every separate European country, a struggle which went through changing fortunes with the rise and fall of democratic revolutions and feudal reactions right through the nineteenth century. The liberation of the Jews became identified with the liberation of the people. The only country which never abrogated the equality of the Jews once it was introduced in 1796 as a result of the French Revolution, was Holland. In its turn, France was the first country where this principle was finally recognized after the July Revolution in 1830. Denmark followed in 1849 and, after prolonged resistance, England in 1858. Ultimately other European countries also granted the Jews lasting equality of rights, in 1867 Austria-Hungary, in 1870 Italy, in 1871 Germany, in 1874 Switzerland, in 1876 Spain, and in 1878 the Balkan states. In Russia the Jews had to wait until the revolution of 1917, and in Rumania even until after World War II. This gradual process of liberation owed much to the vigorous ascendancy of industry over agriculture, and of the towns over rural areas.

Thus the European Jews had a sixty-year period, between their emancipation and the advent of national socialism, in which to enjoy full equality of rights with their Christian fellow citizens; and they had in all just over a hundred years of comparative freedom in which to develop. As was only to be expected, the Jews fairly rushed to take advantage of their escape into light and air, of their opportunities for active participation and intellectual development. Suppressed and thwarted for centuries, the vital impulse soared once the yoke of oppression was lifted.

Jews soon fanned out into all professions and occupations. At first, it is true, most of them continued, by sheer force of habit, to pursue what for so long had been the only profession accessible to them and with which they were most familiar—namely, commerce. But while 87 per cent of Jews were occupied in trade and credit activities in Prussia in 1816, and 65 per cent of them likewise in Vienna in 1804, the percentage had fallen to 49.7 in Germany by 1907; in Poland the percentage was 34.6 in 1921; in Czechoslovakia 39.1 the same year; in Amsterdam, where half of all Dutch Jews were concentrated, 39.1 in 1910; and in England, France, Belgium and Italy it was around 40 per cent at the same time. In 1861, twenty-one out of every hundred inhabitants of Prussia employed in commerce were Jews; by 1925, the proportion had fallen to five. In Eastern European countries, a high proportion of Jews continued in their traditional occupations in the crafts and industries, and this proportion indeed increased during the nineteenth century —so much so that the domestic market became too narrow for Jewish craftsmen and great waves of emigration carried them into Western Europe and the United States. As much as 32.2 per cent of Polish Jews in 1921 earned their living in crafts and industry; the figure for Soviet Russia in 1926 was 34.4 per cent (compared with only 19.3 per cent in trade); that for Czechoslovakia in 1921 was 22.7 per cent, and that for Germany in 1907 24.2 per cent—very largely industrial workers.

Relatively the greatest expansion took place in the proportion of Jews entering the free professions; it must be remembered, of course, that in Western Europe it was only after the French Revolution and in Central Europe after the 1820's that Jews had access to the universities and professions. In Germany, the percentage of the Jewish population in the professions became three times the percentage of the non-Jewish population so occupied, and in some branches the disparity was even greater. There were proportionately fifteen times as many Jewish as non-Jewish lawyers, about eight times as many writers and scholars, and about six times as many physicians. There were relatively fewest Jews among schoolteachers and civil servants, because even after the emancipation German and Western European Jews had only limited access to these occupations due to the unconscious persistence of the canon law which forbade giving Jews any sort of power over Christians. In Prussia, for instance, only 0.72 per cent of all schoolteachers were Jews, and only 0.38 per cent of all civil servants. In Poland, on the other hand, where the Jews had their own schools, in 1921 they accounted for 49.3 per cent of all teachers. And in Soviet Russia, where there were no limitations on the public employment of Jews, there were, in 1926, twice and in some places three times as many Jews in government service as corresponded to their proportion in the population. Unlike other countries, Soviet Russia also had proportionately more Jews than non-Jews in the army; in 1926, the proportion of Jews in the Red Army was 2.1 per cent, and their proportion in the total population only 1.8 per cent. Soviet Russia in its first revolutionary period had the distinguishing merit of being the first and only country in the world where anti-Semitism was a criminal offense.

Even farming attracted more Jews, though in this case the expansion was not as vigorous as in other occupations. European agriculture had twenty-six times as many Jewish farmers in 1930-31 as a hundred years earlier, and twice as many as at the beginning of the twentieth century. If the pace of expansion was slower in agriculture than in other occupations, the reason was not, as has often been said, that Jews shun physical labor. The crafts, too, demand physical

labor, and in Palestine the Jews work the land with enthusi-
asm and indeed did so everywhere until the Middle Ages.
The true reason was the estrangement of the Jews from
Europe's country folk and their diffidence with people who
are by nature more conservative, more profoundly addicted
to old customs and prejudices than the more mercurial city
dweller. After all, the Jews were anxious to escape as
quickly as possible from their troubled past and memories.

The integration of the Jews into European social life
was surprisingly swift, hastened on by the desire to forget,
to settle down, to melt into the background. What the
worst tortures of the past could not achieve, namely, the
separation of the Jews from Judaism, now seemed child's
play to the solicitations of a secularized, modern civilization. The Jews embraced not only, as they had done of
old, the cause of humanity, but also the cause of nations.
They were sometimes more nationalistic than their Christian fellow citizens. Large numbers of them accepted
baptism, not always and not only for the sake of their
career and in order to escape the social and conven-
tional barriers which had replaced the former legal ones,
but often out of profound conviction and from the desire to
be wholly absorbed and merged, to disappear as Jews, and
in their turn to yield, to give up everything that could be
adduced against them as grounds of distinction and apart-
ness. They did not realize that baptism came too late, that
all they did with baptism was to answer an accusation from
past epochs, an accusation which had become obsolete with
the waning of the religious influence. The accusations of
the Church could be answered by baptism. The new accusations which now came up could not be answered at all.
Released from the fetters of religious fanaticism, the Jews
were at once caught in the grip of nationalism and of the
capitalist class struggle in nationalistic guise.

Meanwhile the process of assimilation was under way.
The Jewish upper classes mingled socially and intellectually

with the peoples of Europe. The lower classes, which were
gradually rising, were steadily replenished by immigrants
driven westward from the vast reservoirs of Eastern Jewry
by pogroms, poverty or the World War. The Jews in the
upper classes felt disturbed by this accretion, for it kept
reminding them and, even more so, their Christian environment, of the existence of Jewry; it was these immigrants,
they felt, who again and again hampered the process of
their disappearance, of their becoming inconspicuous. Thus
the term "refugee," which in the old days and among gen-
erous men, had been a title of honor, became a term of
abuse. But the assimilated Jews made a mistake; their own
precipitous, over-zealous assimilation, which was a reflec-
tion of their lack of human balance, of their misjudgment
of the right pace and due distance, made them no less conspicuous; it needed no tangible witnesses from the dismal
past. It would have required superhuman self-control and
superhuman wisdom to muster the dispassionate dignity
needful in this delicate situation. How could these things
have been expected of a people that had only just emerged
from centuries of slavery and suppression?

But however the Jews might have behaved, it would have
availed them nothing. Whatever they might have done
would have been turned against them. For they were being
blamed for quite contradictory things, and their achievements were held against them even more than their wrongs.
During the short period of relaxed tension, the Jews did in
point of fact make plentiful contributions in all fields of
human endeavor, and the traces of their activity have left
an indelible mark on the history of modern times. What
they did in trade and industry during that era is far over-
shadowed by their intellectual achievements. And it was
precisely this lively cultural activity of theirs that was
interpreted, to their detriment, as intellectual obtrusiveness,
as a morbid hypertrophy of the mind, even though since
the beginning of this century Jews have been chalking up

no mean successes in sport as well and have shown themselves particularly eager to develop their physical faculties.
The days were past when the Jews were mainly blamed for
their commercial leanings and for their inclination toward
accumulating riches; they were now resented for their ubiq-
uity, because they were felt to be importunate, because they
simply could not be overlooked in any sphere or direction
of human activity. They were condemned equally, and
often in one and the same breath, for their capitalism and
for their socialism, for their patriotism and for their pacifism,
for their Zionism and for their assimilation. To take part in
the life of nations meant taking part also in public life, in
political and social aspirations. Had the Jews stood aside
from public life, which indeed was impossible, this would
surely have been held against them as indifference toward
national problems and as arrogant isolation. As it was, the
Jews were accused of undue interference with the internal
affairs of nations and of exercising a harmful influence.

And thus what had happened so often, happened again.
After a brief, brilliant period, in which the Jews were allowed to take part in the life of the peoples in freedom and
at least outward equality, the clouds of a coming doom
gathered about them. The catastrophe to come was grim-
mer and more terrible than any that preceded it, and there
was no escape. In the past, the religious persecutions, however fearful they were, did at least involve a spiritual conflict; they arose from the belief that the spirit dominates the
body, and that it was possible to escape from them by a
change of spirit, through baptism. What was involved now,
on the other hand, was a physical distinction which was as
irrevocable as it was implacably damning. Everywhere nationalistic movements were also anti-Semitic, and they will
continue to be so as long as they exist, for they draw their
sustenance from the glorification of everything that is one's
own and therefore, implicitly, from the depreciation of what
is another's—and where is factual or attributed otherness

more tangible than in a domestic minority? Nationalism has multiple sources. Emotionally, it is the cheapest satisfaction of a kind of self-esteem that has no other individual gifts to feed on, and which must therefore look for aggrandizement in the exaltation of the native group, of one's own kith and kin. Materially, it is the gilding, the disguising of class and pecuniary interests, which need the flag of an idea, and lately, indeed, of an ideology in order to mobilize the masses in their support and divert the people from dangerous social aspirations. Often the two motivations intermix. But invariably it is the Jews who provide the most convenient foil for self-aggrandizement and the most convenient diversionary target in matters where pecuniary interests are concerned.

German nationalism was quite especially venomous, because it originated in the inferiority complex of a people divided against themselves, never solidly Christianized, and having achieved external unity as late as the nineteenth century, in a world which had long grown too large and complex for the political hegemony of a single nation. These inauspicious foundations and circumstances drove German nationalism into overcompensation, into the absurd extreme of a racial theory pitted not only against other national powers, but against Christianity itself, against its principle of the unity and concord of humanity and against its restraints on the primitive combative instincts. If for no other reason, Jewry appeared to the Nordic race as the arch-enemy on the mere grounds that it was the original seed and exponent of Christianity. This racial theory, with its hatred of the Jews, on the one hand mobilized all the superstitions and aversions which the Christian era had deeply embedded in the people, and all the accusations which had ever been raised against Jewry, including those of the Church; and on the other, it removed the last moral inhibitions which Christianity had, after all, also implanted in the hearts of men. Barely ten years after the Jews had obtained

full equality in Germany, in 1879, the term "anti-Semitism"
appeared for the first time, and with avowed racial conno-
tations, in a petition from Nietzsche's brother-in-law, Bernhard Förster, to the German *Reichstag*. It was then that
racial anti-Semitism entered upon its march of triumph
which was to end in the Third Reich of National Socialism.

From the very beginning the racial theory was a political
instrument, created by the French counts, Boulainvilliers
and Gobineau, to defend the superiority and prerogatives
of the "Germanic" nobility in France against the inferior
"Celts" of the Third Estate. Even these beginnings indicate
the essentially antidemocratic drift of the theory, which, as
developed by Houston Stewart Chamberlain and his followers, led in foreign policy to imperialistic ends.

The Jews, however, stood preponderantly for democracy,
for social equality and for peace, not only because the declaration of human and of civil rights had liberated them,
but also on the basis of their old tradition: their theocracy
and their spiritual law were never compatible with an unlimited claim to human power. Even had this not been the
case—and in fact there have been conservative, nationalistic,
even chauvinistic Jews among European statesmen and
politicians—public opinion would in any event have set the
Jews down as being on the democratic side, if only because
it was there that their emancipation originated.

Furthermore, because of their dispersion throughout
every country, it was always easy to suspect them of international, antipatriotic tendencies and connections. The
Christian conservative parties and governments frequently
used this accusation in their fight against democracy. Thus
in France, the sentence of Captain Dreyfus for treason was
an intrigue of reactionary clerical and monarchist circles
against the republican government. In the year 1905, when
the Russian revolutionary movement threatened to accom-
plish liberal reforms, the forgery of the *Protocols of Zion*
appeared. They were the work of a clerical official of the

Synod and were intended to win the Czar over to terror and pogroms, and to discredit the liberal minister Witte. This document, which introduced to the world the doctrine of the Jewish international conspiracy and its connection with freemasonry, had its effect not in Russia, but in English and German translations. It was taken seriously by the English conservative newspapers and temporarily by Henry Ford in America, but first took on a fateful significance in Germany after World War I, supported by the race theory.

The racial theory is the intellectual expression of a powerful pagan movement. Fundamentally it is the revolt of ancient instincts against the obligations imposed by Christian civilization. As early as the Renaissance the European peoples began to rebel against the uniform, transcendent law of the Church. The growing independence of European rulers and the national legitimation of their struggle for power, the colorful gratifications of worldly life and the manifold rewards of rational enlightenment, of empirical knowledge and technological invention, pushed the influence of Christianity farther and farther into the background.

Yet, even the lay society of that period still recognized, at least in theory, the principles of Christianity as the basis of its civilization. Later, the growing absorption of the human consciousness by economic and technical concerns, the unleashing during World War I of all the lowest human passions, sanctioned by the clergy of each nation, and finally the chaos of the crises that followed, all this made it easy to give way to pagan impulses with a clear conscience—in fact, it wiped out the last remnant of any conscience at all. With the Nazis, paganism freed itself at a stroke of the feeling of sinfulness by means of which the Church had curbed the savage drives; it openly denied the entire basis for this feeling of sin, repudiating the commands of love, human brotherhood and the rest of the decalogue inherited by Christianity. To the modern pagan world the whole of Christian civilization means nothing but a weakening of its elemental instincts. It has reclaimed the right to its wildest passions.

So for the first time since antiquity true Christians suffered, under the rule of the race dogma, the same fate as Jews—with this difference: Christians could still choose whether to be faithful to Christianity or to disown it by innumerable, subtle degrees. For Jews such a choice no longer existed. The dogma of race has made them collectively, biologically culpable. The objective of all former oppressions, expulsions and autos-da-fé was to bring the Jew into the other camp, to make a Christian of him. Now for the first time the intention was to expel and exclude the Jews unconditionally and forever, and that meant ultimately to exterminate them. For the first time the persecution of the Jews was total and world-wide.

Not only was there no longer an escape in baptism, but immigration restrictions and visa controls made it hardly possible for people without means and connections to find a refuge under the protection of a political power. Formerly, when the Jews were driven from one country, there was always another country to take them in. It remained for our times to create an international situation in which Jews had to camp out on a river island between two borders, exposed to the rigors of winter in "No Man's Land," or range the world for weeks in ships that could land them nowhere but in the arms of inevitable torture and death.

Another trap was prepared for the Jews, equally novel and unique. They became the first victims of a paradoxical state of affairs. Technological and economic developments have brought the peoples of the world into a close, inextricable connection. But the moral and mental state of humanity lagged—and lags no less even now—far behind these developments. The nations, wholly unprepared to draw the necessary conclusions and meet the technical interdependence with a true, organizational cooperation, reacted in the old, obsolete manner of strictly following their self-interest.

In such a situation the country which goes to the extreme of selfishness in offense as well as defense, indeed in offense under the guise of defense, necessarily has the advantage. In the attack of the fascist countries against the democracies, the Jews were given a frightful part to play. Formerly when kings and princes expelled their Jews they did so only with a view to internal politics; to seize their fortunes or to divert the troublesome dissatisfaction of the people. The Nazis used the Jews as an instrument of foreign policy. For some time, when they had plundered them thoroughly, they drove them across the borders in raids as lawless and unpredictable as possible, and saddled other countries with the burden of these destitute refugees. There, in the foreign countries the refugees were awaited by fascist agitators who roused the population to anger against them, using Jew-baiting to stir up the masses against their own democratic government. Everywhere, round the nucleus of Jew-baiting, gathered groups sympathetic toward fascism.

Here the doctrine of the international conspiracy of the Jews could be used to the best advantage, for it permitted of the most contradictory applications. Finance is international, so is communism; pacifist endeavors are international, and so is the resentment of the Jews against the persecutors, hence Jewish warmongering. "International" is equivalent to "unpatriotic," "antinational," and "rootless." To take effect, these catchwords need not be logically connected, they have merely to be thrown in now and then, according to the specific audiences, when pointing to some weaknesses in the body politic. This new technique of using Judaism as a weapon in the international struggle not only charged the Jews with guilt, it compelled them to be instrumental in the disruption of democracy. At the same time it made the democratic countries, which refused asylum to the refugees, into accomplices of the Nazi crime.

The Jews, on the average, are no worse and no better than

other peoples. And yet there is something which distinguishes them, and that is the magnitude of the demands which their God, or their destiny, or their aspiration, whatever we may call it, has made upon them; demands which they have never relinquished, yet have never been able to fulfill. This has caused them to suffer more than all other peoples, and the more they are made to suffer, the greater the distinction conferred upon them. Such an excess of suffering through thousands of years must carry a special historic significance. But here we face the bounds where understanding ends and faith begins.

Translated from the German by
Alexander and Elizabeth Henderson

The Jews and the Germans

IT IS NOT, after the experiences of our age, so easy to view the relations between Germans and Jews with calm and equanimity, not as easy for us as for governments which, for reasons of expediency, "let bygones be bygones."

We cannot and we must not forget what happened. But we can and indeed we should try to probe the roots of the events, honestly and soberly, in order to gain distance from them and to alleviate our haunting memories. Not only the Germans, but the Jews as well must make such attempts to purify and clarify their minds; for what happens to somebody is just as much part of his being as what he does. How could we in a world like ours, a world of mounting confusion and recklessness, of continually impending mass extermination, keep our senses intact without keeping events at bay by efforts to cool our minds and hold on to our reason.

From the outset it should be stated that what happened in Germany is not entirely a matter of German-Jewish relations. A wider perspective of recent developments has made us aware of the fact that those monstrosities form part of an overall trend in our unfortunate epoch, a trend toward progressive overcivilized dehumanization. It is, however, no accident that this trend has found its most radical, its first completely and deliberately ruthless expression in the German treatment of the Jews. Such an extraordinary way of dealing with human beings cannot simply be attributed to that general rise of mechanical mass destruction which started in the First World War and is a consequence of technological progress and the indifference toward human life and suffering that goes with it. Nor can it be explained by the various pandemic motivations of anti-Judaism as they have been propounded in so many psychological and sociological studies of the phenomenon.

To be sure, anti-Judaism arose far back in antiquity and has persisted ever since all over the Western world, with more or less open virulence. Its overt causes are manifold, but they can, all of them, be traced back, directly or indirectly, to the peculiar, transnational existence and persistence of the Jewish people. We should not, as it is too often done, represent ourselves as mere victims, and it is unworthy of our tradition and unjustified by our history to interpret Judaism in terms of Passion and passivity only. There has been at the core of the Jewish people an unshakeable will to affirm their special, quasi-constitutional idea of humanity, to affirm it in all circumstances, in religious as well as in secular terms. The concept of man as created in the image of God, of a metaphysical, ideological God, purified of any anthropomorphic relations, and impeccable at the expense of man who forever strives and fails to live up to His demands—this concept carried from the beginning the seeds of all the mundane devotions of the Jews and of the resentment which these were bound to arouse. The representation of unrepresentable, spiritual, though intimately personal, divinity, became the abiding life principle of Judaism. Even the bad qualities of the Jews—of which there are plenty—are only the reverse of this idea.

The first pogroms occurred in the second century, B.C., in Alexandria under the Ptolemies—indeed they were instigated by Ptolemy VII—and in Palestine under the Seleucid, Antiochus Epiphanes. Just like these Hellenistic rulers, the Romans, too, had great trouble with the refractory Jews,

who stubbornly resisted being lured or coerced into inter-
fusing in the common civilizational melting pot. It was the
same peculiarity—the adherence to the revelation of a spiritual, universal God, their very possession of such a revelation—that made the Jews a proselyting, magnetic power
and, on the other hand, an "*odium generis humani,*" an
abomination to mankind.

So, anti-Judaism existed even in the pagan world. But
there is a fundamental difference between this early anti-
Judaism and the later anti-Judaism initiated and perpetuated by the Christian Church. Pagans and Jews were quite
unrelated; they conflicted on the same level. In fact, one
could almost say that the Jews were indistinctly felt to
possess a mysteriously superior power by virtue of their
imperturbably clinging to an invisible, mysterious deity.
What people resented was their "arrogance," their refusal to
conform and to mingle with the easygoing crowd. Christianism, however, was connected with Judaism by an intri-
cate, indissoluble bond. Judaism was the source of Christianity, spiritually as well as genetically: *spiritually,* for the
teachings and the Messianic role of Jesus were the final out-
growth of Jewish prophecy, and the Christian doctrine of
original sin, the basis of the Church's power of absolution,
depended on the Jewish history of creation; *genetically,*
because the first Christian communities abroad issued from
groups of Jewish proselytes, the Greek *sebomenoi,* worship-
pers of the Jewish God. In an almost unbroken transition,
Jewish tradition passed over into Christian tradition,
Jewish proselytism into Christian proselytism, Jewish martyrdom into Christian martyrdom, Christianity into Christology. And internally, within the Judaeo-Christian orbit, the
same situation of conflict developed as had prevailed
between pagans and Jews: again the Jews rejected the concept of an incarnate deity, with all its basically pagan
implications; and again they were accused of unyielding
obstinacy—but now by their own, equally zealous offspring,

by a religious creed which had an undetachable share in Jewish destiny.

Paradoxically, the old pagan resentments were resuscitated by a fanaticism of the Jewish kind, all the more violent because of the kinship. Since Christianity was forever unable to rid itself of its Jewish inheritance, this relationship itself was turned into an instrument of embittered severance. The Jews were represented as the murderers of God. According to Paul, the sacrificial death of Christ was preordained; God the Father had willed it and had blinded the Jews, in order to bring it about. The Jews were to bear this curse until the end of time. Augustine decreed the role of the Jews in the Christian world; other Christian Fathers and scholars, Thomas Aquinas for one, reiterated the execration: like Cain, the Jews must not be destroyed, they must be preserved, forever to serve as witnesses of the Christian truth; they must live on as perpetual servants to the Christian peoples (*"Ecce Judaeus servus est Christiani"*).

This vehement hostility of the Christian Church was the basis of all subsequent anti-Judaism. All persecutions, restrictions, exclusions, economic, social, political, all degradation and humiliation which the Jews underwent in the Western world, may be traced back to this spiritually parricidal Christian repudiation of Judaism, which spread with the expanding power of the Church. Even the atrocities of the anti-Christian Nazis would not have been possible without the millennial picture of the Jew, created, spiritually and bodily, by the Christian Church. What I say here is a statement of fact. But we should accept our share in this happening. What lies at the bottom of it all is, as I have indicated, the unique, metaphysically physical cohesion of the Jews, their intransigent holding fast to their idea by means of a legalistic ritual that survived and supplanted their forfeited statehood.

Jewish history throughout the Christian era has been

one of continuous expulsions, restrictions, exclusions, and shameless exploitation. But with all this, including the stakes and massacres, hostility did not reach that climactic point of a deliberate attempt at wholesale extermination, such as our generations were condemned to experience in Nazi Germany. While the Church was compelled to preserve the Jews because of her Jewish ancestry, the Nazis had no such inhibitions. On the contrary, they extended their persecution to the Jewish-informed Christian values. But why did anti-Judaism, in our generally secularized era, reach that climax precisely in Germany? The Jews had been popular scapegoats all along and everywhere, for obvious reasons. Whenever something went wrong, the rulers found it convenient to divert the anger of the people to the Jews, but never and nowhere to such extremes.

Apart from the general trend toward recklessness in our time, which I have just mentioned, we have certainly to take into account the extremities to which the Germans were driven by their defeat and the insensate treatment they endured at the hands of the Western powers after the war. All this, however, does not suffice for a thorough explanation. There are certain historical residues in the German mentality which were brought to the fore by the situation of distress, a very special relationship between Germans and Jews, a psychic and mental interpenetration which, I contend, played a decisive role in the events. Just as the intrinsic relationship of Christianity to Judaism was a primal incentive to the Christian subjugation of the Jews, so, on the other end of the arc of history, the special relationship between Germans and Jews was a prominent factor in the atrocious excesses of the Third Reich.

A peculiar affinity between the two peoples has frequently been observed by discerning minds, Jewish and non-Jewish. Let me quote first two outstanding Germans: "Germany is nothing," Goethe said, "but the Germans are much; and yet, the Germans hold just the contrary to be true. They should be transplanted and dispersed all over the globe, like the Jews. Only then could they develop all the good that is in them for the benefit of all nations." And in his diary he notes: "Germans will never vanish, like the Jews, because they are, all of them, individuals." Stefan George, in his "Stern des Bundes" (1914), stated the relationship even more poignantly:

Ihr Äußerste von windumsauster klippe
Und schneeiger brache! Ihr von glühender wüste!
Stammort des gott-gespenstes . . . gleich entfernte
Von heitrem meer und Binnen, wo sich leben
Zu ende lebt in welt von gott und bild! . . .
Blond oder schwarz, demselben schoß entsprungne
Verkannte Brüder, suchend euch und hassend,
Ihr immer schweifend und drum nie erfüllt!

[You, the extremes: the one from barren snow-drifts
And wave-swept cliffs, the other from the desert,
Place of a spectral God. Remote alike
From seas and lands serene, where mortals may
Live out their lives among their imaged Gods.
Fair-haired or dark, the selfsame womb begot you
Who hate and seek and do not know the brother
You, always roaming, ever unfulfilled.]

On the Jewish side, in 1880 Ludwig Bamberger remarked: "To no other people have the Jews grown so close [*haben sich so zusammengelebt*] as they have to the Germans. They are Germanized not only on German soil, far beyond the German boundaries. . . . There must be correspondences in the basic disposition [of the two peoples] which made Germany and all things German particularly attractive for the Jews, and the Jews an especially useful complement to the German character." [1] And, in 1911,

---

[1] *Deutschtum und Judentum,* 1880.

Moritz Goldstein wrote: "In spite of persecution, derision, and disdain, a common existence of a thousand years has so deeply interwoven Jewish with German life, that a disengagement would seem impossible." [2] Well, twenty years later, a cruel surgery made it possible.

These are just indications, significant enough, of something that happened between Jews and Germans, particularly in the last two centuries; a dramatic dialectical exchange on both sides, touching the nerve of existence. Let us look a little closer at this ambivalently intense relationship.

As a result of the French Revolution, the general emancipation of the Jews got underway all over the West; it went on, gradually advancing, despite repeated reverses. In the Latin countries it was mainly the rulers who attempted to stem the tide. In France, Napoleon, by his famous "infamous decree" of 1808, temporarily and quite ineffectually restricted the Jewish civil rights which had been established in 1791; popular protests against the emancipation came only from the German provinces. In Italy, it was Pope Pius VII who, after the downfall of Napoleon, abolished the liberation and restored the ghettos and the inquisition. In England, the ruling classes in Parliament delayed the establishment of Jewish equality of status by devious means, like the insistence, until 1858, on the Christian oath of allegiance for Members of Parliament. But nowhere in the West, neither in the Latin countries nor in England, did the emancipation of the Jews become such a burning question, nowhere did it arouse such violent emotions, indeed physical outbursts, as in Germany. Generally, anti-Jewish feelings were motivated by religious or economic factors: the Jew was the hardened negator, indeed killer of the Lord, or the financial master, exploiter, usurer—both images being the doctrinal and factual results of a millennial Chris-

[2] "Deutsch-jüdischer Parnass," in *Kunstwart*, 1912.

tian enslavement. The German resentment against the Jews, however, reached very early the stage of racial and characterological hostility. Anti-Judaism turned into anti-Semitism. National Socialism has a long, prominent ancestry in Germany, from the beginning to the end of the nineteenth century: from Grattenauer (1803), Fichte, Ruehs, and Fries to Richard Wagner, Stoecker, Duehring, Bernhard Foerster, Wilhelm Marr, and Lagarde; and further on to Langbehn, Wahrmund, Ahlwardt, Theodor Fritsch, Kunze, Klages, and Schuler; from the Hep-Hep movement of 1819 to the boycott of Jewish shops in 1890 and 1891, and the Buschhof ritual murder trial of 1892. Anti-Semitism as an *organized* force—that is to say anti-Semitic leagues, congresses, manifestos and parties—originated in Germany.

But just as striking and exceptional is the reverse: the peculiar affinity between Germans and Jews, the correspondence and interpenetration of their destinies. While friction with Jews was less in the West, and practically nonexistent in modern Italy and Spain before the fascist era, we could neither find in these countries such deep and fecund personal relations, such mutual intellectual and emotional sparking between Jews and non-Jews as between Moses Mendelssohn, Lessing, and Lavater, between Markus Herz and Kant, David Friedländer and the Humboldts, Schleiermacher and Henriette Herz, Jean Paul and Emanuel Osmund (the only salient parallel in the West that occurs to me is the friendship between Péguy and Bernard-Lazare). These are just the most conspicuous among many such ties of affection, tested in the most perilous circumstances, as I myself have seen and experienced them.

In France and in England the economic prominence of Jews grew with the nineteenth century. Jewish bankers, particularly, came to play an important role. The political and cultural developments of these nations, however, followed their own national course, hardly touched by any specifically Jewish influence. But viewing the train of events in Germany since the end of the eighteenth century, we cannot help being amazed at the deep and continuing effects of Jewish activity on German affairs in nearly every domain.

In the Western countries cultural and intellectual leadership rested traditionally with the national aristocracies who, with their airy minds and manners, were always at the forefront of the epoch. The intellectual commerce which in France took place in the *"bureaux d'esprit"*—the intellectual salons—of aristocratic ladies, had in Germany its center among Jewish women. Long before the political and social equality of the Jews was established by law, the elite of the Enlightenment and the romantic movement gathered in the Berlin houses of the Mendelssohns and Veits, of Henriette Herz and Rahel Varnhagen, and in Vienna around the Arnsteins and Eskeles. Even Jew-baiters like E. T. A. Hoffmann and the dean and "Oberkonsistorialrat" Teller frequented these Jewish circles. As Henriette Herz stated in her memoirs, "the Christian houses offered nothing equivalent, or similar, to Jewish intellectual company and sociability. . . . A Christian middle class with interests other than those suggested by their profession did not exist at that time. . . . The high officials and officers shared the currently sanctioned trends of the court to which they mostly belonged by their noble birth, and which entirely lacked an intellectually stimulating social life. . . . Small wonder that those who sought intellectual advancement through personal exchange of ideas eagerly seized the opportunity of such company, in spite of all the prevailing prejudices against Jews. . . . As if by magic these circles attracted all young people of intellectual eminence who lived in Berlin or visited it." [3]

And here is a letter which Friedrich von Gentz, the politician, publicist, and confidant of Metternich, wrote from Vienna in 1802 to his friend Karl Gustav von Brinkmann:

[3] Henriette Herz, *Erinnerungen*, ed. J. Fürst (Berlin, 1958), p. 121.

". . . The house of the Arnsteins, which alone offers me some compensation for the Viennese annoyances, this house is the amplest, and in some respects the only resource of all the foreigners arriving in Vienna, and an invaluable one for those who, like me, are entitled to claim help and friendship through older connections with Berlin and Jewish affairs, which all of us have looked down upon, and which I now venerate on my knees [*"im Staube verehre"*]. How good I felt when I met here, on one and the same spot, besides your lovable friend Henrietta [Pereira, née von Arnstein], with her exquisite mother [Fanny von Arnstein], also Mad. Levi, whom I have always liked and thought much of, Mad. Ephraim, whom—shame on me—I had never so much as looked at, and whom I now consider one of the most interesting women I have ever met, Mad. Eskeles, about whom I often teased you, Frau von Eybenberg [Goethe's friend], who is my comfort, friend and support here, and, in the company of all these intelligent, good-natured and praiseworthy women, all that is alive, companionable and tolerable in Vienna. This house is in more than one sense a little world. Without it, I would have left Vienna long ago; with it, one cannot despair completely, dreadful, though everything else may be." [4]

It should be noted that this Jewish service of social crystallization of the intelligentsia was an additional incentive, absent in other countries, to anti-Jewish attacks. The very intelligence of the Jews that was sought as intellectual stimulant stirred the resentment against them. "This precisely is the deadly sin of the Jews," the same Gentz wrote

[4] From *Juden und Judentum in deutschen Briefen aus drei Jahrhunderten,* ed. Franz Kobler (Vienna, 1935), pp. 147 ff. Gentz's *"brouillerie"* with Fanny von Arnstein, which occurred a year later, and his subsequent anti-Semitic utterances do not diminish the significance of this enthusiastic depiction of the whole Jewish circle.

later, "intelligence they all have, more or less, but he is yet
to be born in whom a spark of feeling can be found." [5]
Politically, Jews played a more momentous role in Germany than in any other European nation. It was, of course,
only natural that Jews stood in the forefront of the fight
for *democracy, liberalism* and *constitutional government*,
since in this fight their own civil betterment was involved.
But beyond that and with particular eagerness the German
Jews identified their own with purely German concerns.
Eduard von Simson, President of the revolutionary Frankfurt National Assembly, and later of the North German and
the first Imperial *Reichstag* and of the first German *Reichs-
gericht* (Supreme Court), Gabriel Riesser, Vice-president
of the National Assembly, Eduard Lasker, cofounder and
leader of the National Liberal Party, and Ludwig Bamberger, adviser of Bismarck and the Emperor Frederick
III—all of them were prominent champions of German unification. Simson, in his capacity as president of the *Reichstag*, was the leader of the parliamentary deputation which,
in 1870, offered the King of Prussia the imperial crown.
Friedrich Julius Stahl was the theoretical founder and
political leader of the Prussian and German *Conservative
Party*, and initiator of the Prussian Chamber of Lords
(*Herrenhaus*). Another Jewish convert who exerted considerable influence on conservative ideology was Johann
August Wilhelm Neander, Professor of Protestant Theology
at the University of Berlin. As to the *Socialist movement*,
I need not stress the predominance among its founders of
the German Jews, Ferdinand Lassalle and Karl Marx, and of
the many Jewish leaders of the German socialist parties
during the last century, who fought, suffered, and died for
the idea.

So we find Jews at the fountainhead of the three main
trends of German political life in the last century: liberalism, conservatism, socialism. And beyond party lines, Jew-

[5] Letter to Brinkmann, September 19, 1804, *ibid.*, p. 149.

ish political writers kept stirring German public opinion,
as did for instance Ludwig Boerne, or Maximilian Harden,
the partisan and confidant of Bismarck and violent oppo-
nent of William II. There is hardly a Jewish figure in the
Western and Southern countries who could match all these
German Jews in political importance, with the exception of
Benjamin Disraeli in England, and, perhaps, the French
antagonists, Georges Mandel and Léon Blum.

Commercial activities of the Jews, for more than a millennium the only means of escape from restriction and servi-
tude, were burgeoning everywhere in the nineteenth
century. They were more predominant in Germany because
of the splintered state of the country, the *Kleinstaaterei,* and
in it the backwardness of the feudal authorities. Every
ruler of the many principalities had his Jewish court factor
administering his financial affairs and, with the developing
statehood of the principalities, the court factors turned into
independent bankers. (The founding Rothschild, for instance, started as court factor in Hesse.) Just as the provincial courts in Germany were incapable of, indeed
adverse to, fostering intellectual life, in the same way, and
for the same reasons, they did not, with the exception of
Prussia, provide their population with the scope and the
encouragement for commercial pursuits. So the Jews, in their
very capacity as outcasts and outsiders, were the first to
occupy key financial positions, to set up banks and international trading, using their connections abroad. While
they rendered valuable services by introducing modern
forms of financial enterprise, the commercial activities of
some of them in the disruptive period of the 1920's were
certainly, like those of quite a number of Gentiles, of a
dubious sort.

At crucial turning points of twentieth-century German
history, Jews played decisive parts. The Jew Walther
Rathenau organized the German raw material supply in
the First World War and originated modern planned econ-

omy. As Minister of Foreign Affairs, he was the one who, by concluding the Rapallo treaty with Russia broke through the political confinement of Germany after the war. It was, alas, the Jewish chemist, Fritz Haber, who inaugurated the German chemical war industry. A Jew, Kurt Eisner, was the first to overthrow a German monarchy, and thereby he actually started what goes under the name of the German Revolution of 1918. In this revolutionary process, two deeply humane human beings, Rosa Luxemburg and Gustav Landauer, had leading roles. All four of them, Rathenau, Eisner, Rosa Luxemburg, and Landauer, paid for this leadership with their lives.

At the other extreme, the Jew Albert Ballin killed himself out of sheer grief over the German collapse. And hardly any record of the paradoxical role the Jews played in this German crisis is as touchingly revealing as a passage from the very outspoken memoir of John Meynard Keynes, member of the British delegation at the Peace Conference in Versailles in 1919, about his opposite German delegate, the Jew Dr. Carl Melchior, the only one in the German delegation who, in Keynes's words, "upheld the dignity of defeat." In a private meeting of the two men after the event, Keynes relates:

". . . he told me of the last days at Weimar, and the struggle over the signature of the Treaty, his own resignation, how these days had been the most dreadful of all, how Erzberger had deliberately betrayed to an agent of the English Government the decision of a secret Cabinet Meeting between Noske, David, and himself [Erzberger], in which it had been decided that in any event they must sign, and how he, Melchior, believed that it was out of a knowledge of this decision that Lloyd George finally decided to abandon his efforts toward moderation. Melchior's emotions were towards Germany and the falsehood and humiliation which his own people had brought on themselves, rather than towards us. . . . The breach of promise, the breach of discipline, the decay of honourable behaviour, the betrayal of undertakings by the one party and the insincere acceptance by the other of impossible conditions which it was not intended to carry out, Germany almost as guilty to accept what she could not fulfil as the Allies to impose what they were not entitled to exact—it was these offences against The Word—the Tablets of the Law—which so much wounded him. . . . German honour and organisation and morality were crumbling; he saw no light anywhere; he expected . . . civilisation to grow dim . . . dark forces were passing over us." [6]

In this attitude of a lone Jewish peace delegate standing for Germany more forthrightly and intransigently than the Germans themselves, and doing so as, in the words of Keynes, "a strict and upright moralist, a worshipper of the tablets of the Law, a Rabbi," in the attitude of this man we have the tragic image of the Jew, merging with his foreign home country to the point of passionately desired identity, and yet remaining what he could not help being, the ineffaceable Jew.

Finally, the special attraction to all things German manifests itself in the intense Jewish relationship to the language and the land. It began early: the Yiddish language, which is spoken by Orthodox Jews even in non-German countries, in England and America, in Russia and Poland, is based on Middle High German; the relationship culminates in the literary preeminence of modern German Jews, which equals their conspicuousness in political life. Again, with the one exception of Marcel Proust, we find in the Western and Southern countries no Jewish poet or literary artist of the

[6] J. M. Keynes, *Two Memoirs* (New York and London, 1949), pp. 50, 69 ff.

stature of Heine, of the poets of the Young Vienna circle, of Kafka, Wolfskehl, Hermann Broch, Karl Kraus, nor even of Werfel, Doeblin and many other outstanding Jewish expressionists. Kafka's prose belongs to the most beautiful, classically beautiful, German prose ever written. The meticulous precision and subtle pliancy of the style of Karl Kraus, his satirically preceptorial attention to the purity of the language has no parallel among European Jewry. And even after the catastrophe, the lyrical records of defiant parting, the laments and elegies of Karl Wolfskehl, Else Lasker-Schueler, Nelly Sachs, Paul Celan, Gertrud Kolmar, are great German poetry. The congenial symbiosis of Jewish and German, indeed Germanic disposition, is uniquely represented in the figure of Karl Wolfskehl. Although he emphasized his exile and his biblical rootage more strongly than any other refugee, turning as he did to New Zealand, "the Antipodes," and passionately professing the word of the God of Israel, he could not eradicate the German part of his being, grown through a millennial Rhenish ancestry, he could not extinguish his nostalgia, of which his fierce existential protest was in itself a marked expression. The German émigré, Erich Maria Remarque, hit an ironical truth with the answer he is said to have given to a Nazi emissary who wooed him with the promise of the highest honors if he would be willing to return to Germany. When he refused, the Nazi asked him: "Are you not a bit homesick?" "Homesick?" Remarque said, "No. I am not Jewish."

What we have contemplated so far is the sad spectacle of the Jews pressing, or being pressed so deeply into German existence as to provoke violent repulsion. "German Jewry perished," Bernhard Guttmann said, "because it did not stay alien enough. Its *hubris* consisted in the desire to assimilate completely."[7]

[7]*Schattenriß einer Generation (1888–1919)* (Stuttgart, 1950), pp. 238 ff.

But this is only half of the process. Matters were not so simple. It was not that an unequivocal Jewish eagerness to be integrally German was plainly confronted with a German urge to get rid of the obtrusive, never quite assimilable element in German life. The situation was complicated by reverse currents on both sides. There existed a peculiar German philo-Semitism, and there existed also a profound Jewish aversion to a certain strain in the German character, which, for historical reasons to be specified presently, has become overpowerful in recent times.

I have mentioned the intense personal relationships between Germans and Jews that developed even before the establishment of Jewish civil rights. In these bonds of friendship a strong emphasis of sentiment can be discerned on the German side. Exemplary witnesses to German philo-Semitism are Lessing who wrote *Nathan der Weise*, a monument to the noble Jew, and Nietzsche, whose work is filled with praise of the Jews, aware as he was of Jewish flaws. "What a blessing a Jew is among Germans!" he exclaimed. He got so emotional over anti-Semitism that he wanted anti-Semites expelled from Germany. From the experience of my own lifetime I could produce quite a number of instances of a special predilection of Germans for the Jewish kind. I mention just one, a droll one.

In my student days at Heidelberg the editor of the Heidelberg newspaper, Wildhagen, was a prominent figure in our Café Häberlein. He could be found there regularly in the evening in the company of Jewish students and scholars, playing chess or participating in intellectual discussions. One night—it was St. John's day, midsummer day, when the student corps and fraternities used to stage a bonfire on the square in front of the university, performing their rites in full regalia, and there was much drinking and rioting everywhere—Mr. Wildhagen had already left the café to go home, when all of a sudden he reappeared and shouted through the room: "Herr Cohn, please escort me home. The *goi* is loose."

Here we have a very revealing situation: the ominous word is pronounced by a German gentile, a thoroughly friendly individual, siding with the Jews and apparently aroused to the same feelings as are the Jews in the face of such happenings. Other Germans, however, felt the sting of this word, felt it aimed at them in hostility and arrogant contempt; and there is a certain justification for this feeling. We have to be candid and clear on this point.

Goyim means literally Latin *gentes, gentiles*—hence in English, "gentiles"—"the peoples," that is, the foreign peoples, with the ancient connotation of "heathens," the ones who do not believe in the biblical universal God. It has the same meaning as the *gentiles* against whom the Church Fathers and scholars directed their *summae*. But, gradually, the Jewish word *goi* (or *goy*) assumed a more restricted significance; in its very implication of heathenry it took on a secularized, more specific, and at the same time broader and deeper, purport. *Goyim*, in its modern usage, no longer means gentiles pure and simple, that is, *all* gentiles; it means *certain* gentiles, *certain* Germans, a specific type, a specific mode of life and inclinations. For a clarification of this meaning of the word *goi*, its innuendos and the peculiar flavor it has in Jewish idiom, we have to delve a little deeper into the historical roots of the connection and division between Germans and Jews.

As factual evidence has indicated, the relationship between these two peoples is one of profound affinity and profound difference. What unites them is, above all, that they are both transnational peoples, each, however, in a distinct and in fact antagonistic sense. The Jews, in the early stages of their history, transcended their earthly statehood, their community of land and language; they transcended it once and for all by becoming a global people, dispersed, but in their dispersion coherent, ritually and spiritually. Historical processes are irreversible, and, as indispensable and admirable as modern Israel certainly is, never again can the whole Jewish people, neither its physical being, nor its spiritual scope, be squeezed back into this belated little modern state. The Jews did not live through two millennia of a world-scale destiny, fraught with meaning and ineffable experience, to end up within a tiny nationalistic framework.

The Germans are transnational in the opposite sense: they have never achieved a true, homogeneous national community and seem to have been predestined for this tragic failure. Even the shallow national unification which they reached as late as 1871, after a thousand years of striving and laboring, was lost again in 1945. Down through the centuries German poets and thinkers have bewailed this predicament. "Germany?" Schiller asked in his *Xenien*, "But where is it, I cannot discover this country./ Where the learned begins, the political ends." And again: "You Germans are striving in vain to form yourselves into a nation./ Try to bring up in yourselves free human beings instead." [8] And remember Goethe's dictum which I have already quoted; "Germany is nothing, but the Germans are much. . . . They should be . . . dispersed all over the globe, like the Jews" to bring out the good in them.

The Jews were originally, and essentially still are, a tribe, that is to say, an ethnic community formed by and rooted in a religion, a religion of its own—in contradistinction to a nation, which is a community founded on secular grounds against the background of a world religion, a community of land and language, customs and traditions. The ritualistic

[8]Das deutsche Reich: *Deutschland? Aber wo liegt es? Ich weiß das Land nicht zu finden./Wo das gelehrte beginnt, hört das politische auf.* Deutscher Nationalcharakter: *Zur Nation euch zu bilden, ihr hoffet es, Deutsche vergebens./Bildet, ihr könnt es, dafür freier zu Menschen euch aus!*

conduct of life, the quasi-physical, unflinching adherence to the ritual—a rather primitive trait—was the bodily support of the Jews, which sustained them through all the tribulations of the ages. Even today, among thoroughly secularized and assimilated Jews one may find, in certain atavisms, compulsion neuroses, dietary sensitivities, the traces of the former ritualistic life. Yet, the Jewish people would have perished long ago if their religion, the substance and substratum of the ritual, had been a plainly particularistic one like the many pagan cults of antiquity, all of which disappeared or were absorbed by world religions. The saving, yet tragic, peculiarity of Judaism consisted in the combination of tribal ritual and a religious doctrine, which from its early stages aimed at universality and spirituality, one implying the other. Judaism, persisting in particularity, insisted on universality—particularism and universalism helped each other along. In this way the Jews were enabled eventually, in a secularized era, to break through the ritualistic barriers, and, marked as they were by the imprint of an age-old particularity, to dedicate themselves to universal causes, internationalism and supranationalism in any form: liberalism, capitalism, socialism, pacifism. This is why, in a nationalistic epoch, the Jews were accused of a stubborn, ethnic cohesion among themselves and, at the same time, of international, or supranational activities, both of which suggest an antinational attitude.

This paradoxical situation of the Jews in the modern era was aggravated by another, equally paradoxical circumstance. Excluded as they were for many centuries from the common life of the peoples around them, expelled and hounded from one country to the other, and actually living on the chimerical grounds of their biblical world, they were, after their release from the ghettos, only too eager to become rooted in a terrestrial homeland and to identify their destinies with those of this homeland. But their self-denial, their forced, overcompensatory loyalty could never quite extinguish their Jewish aura, especially in Germany where Christian anti-Judaism turned into racial anti-Semitism. Rathenau, a super-German Jew, indeed Germany's liberator from the fetters imposed on her by the Western powers, was killed by the nationalists. And Dr. Melchior, in his moment of deepest devotion to Germany, made the impression of a rabbi.

With such natural and historical predisposition the Jews had to face a German situation which was the result of a diametrically opposite course of history. While the *Jews* had made their way from an ancient tribal kingdom toward an intangible universal community, *from particularity to universality*, the *Germans* had started from a universal framework, the Holy Roman Empire, and their repeated, ever abortive efforts were directed toward the achievement of a concrete, homogeneous national community. They were moving *from universality toward particularity*.

In the Middle Ages, the Germanic rulers, made Roman emperors, were incapable of keeping their rival peers in bounds. Perpetually torn between the attempted control of the anarchy at home and the defense of their imperial authority abroad, they spent their energies and properties without succeeding in either of these overtaxing endeavors. They were unable to establish a supreme dynasty lasting long enough to take roots in the country, to build a national tradition and a leading society; no permanent, residential capital could evolve. The nobility, instead of gathering around the emperor, kept behaving like his peers. Warring, or residing on their manorial estates, they refused urbanization until very late and preserved traces of their anticivilizational and anti-intellectual boorishness well into the modern age. The ensuing anarchy resulted in the much deplored *Kleinstaaterei*, the lasting division of the country into a multitude of most diverse provincial governments and principalities, which was an unconquerable obstacle to its unification. Consequently, a fateful rift developed between the political and intellectual spheres—"Where the learned begins, the political ends," as Schiller put it.

German intellectual life did not issue from court society, but from the middle class of the provincial cities, which took over from the clerics the care of education and learning. The important minds in Germany lacked the experience of a national style of life which might have spontaneously informed their concepts. They had to derive their theories from abstract, purely speculative principles. Generations of great German thinkers and poets, from Leibniz to Kant, Lessing, Herder, Schiller, Goethe, and the romanticists, searched for a universally valid order of things and concerned themselves with Germany only in bemoaning her wretched condition. And when in the nineteenth century the Napoleonic conquests had finally ridded the country of the ghostly Holy Roman Empire, the forces that finally accomplished an actual German Reich were not those who had set the aims, the progressive, universal-minded idealists and romanticists of the Wars of Liberation. Unification was achieved by the pressure of economic interests and the Prussian power drive. In the German Reich of 1871, the universalism, humanism, and democratic progressivism of the intelligentsia was scorned by the ruling classes, that is, the military and the officialdom, which were dominated by the Junkers and their inveterate hostility to intellect. Intellect was identified with anti-nationalism, anti-patriotism, and unconcern with the national aggrandizement that was pursued to overcompensate an age-old frustration. The extreme manifestation of this attitude was the Nazis' hatred and persecution of the intelligentsia, the "*Intelligenzbestien.*"

"The patriotism of the Frenchman," Heine wrote in *Die romantische Schule 1833*, "warms and expands his heart so that it embraces with its love not only his close relatives, but the whole of France, indeed the whole of civilization.

The patriotism of the German, on the contrary, consists in
a narrowing of his heart, which contracts like leather in
the cold so that he comes to hate all that is foreign and no
longer wants to be a cosmopolite, a European, but merely
and plainly a petty German. Thus we witnessed . . . the
mean and coarse opposition to that lofty spirit that is
precisely the most glorious, the most sacred thing which
Germany has produced, opposition to that humanism, cos-
mopolitism, human brotherhood, to which our great minds,
Lessing, Herder, Schiller, Goethe, Jean Paul and all cultivated Germans have always adhered."

What happened after the First World War, when again
the champions of social and human brotherhood failed and
were let down by the Western powers, was a savage revolt
of the body against the intellect, of physical drives against
the aims of the mind. And the Jews, who had reached their
civil equality in the very period of rising nationalism and
anti-intellectualism, overzealous as they were to prove
themselves German to the full, to support, to take part in
all German endeavors, but unable completely to quell their
intellectual and supranational inclinations—the Jews met
this brutish revolt head on.

This latent quality in the German, *this potential of
becoming arrested and immured in his own body, this
emphasis on brute force,* it is this which the Jews always
sensed and could not help detesting, and it is, in return,
this special aversion, which the physical Germans could not
help resenting in Jews. It is precisely this which the word
goi means to the Jews, and what the word aroused in the
Germans. The Jews were extremely devoted to the Germans of the other kind, to those Germans whom a nationally
unfortunate history had pushed beyond the narrow national
frame and who had been made particularly capable of
identifying their national quality with humanity proper,
with a comprehensiveness of aim that transcends the national self; those Germans who tend toward reconciliation

and synthesis of divergent national styles of life, and whom
Schiller had in mind when he said that "the day of the
Germans will be the harvest of all times." The Jews were
constitutionally close to the type of alert, cultivated, open-
minded, and open-hearted Germans who are self-critical
and self-ironical just as the Jews are. But they were irre-
pressively hostile to that opposite type of German, in whom
German history produced an ineradicable inferiority complex, a persecution complex; who could not overcome bit-
terness about Germany's having missed her hegemonial
day, the glory of predominance that all the Western nations
have enjoyed, and who projected the national failure outward, at the expense of other peoples. The mythical im-
personators of this self-image are *der reine Tor, Siegfried,*
the trustful hero who was stabbed in the back, and most
particularly *der deutsche Michel,* the good, honest, naive
simpleton wearing a nightcap to indicate his drowsiness, his
sluggishness. He is the one who always gets it in the neck,
who is constantly cheated and outwitted, by the perfidious
British (*das perfide Albion*), the treacherous French and
Italians, and especially by the tricky Jews. Unfit to cope
with this ubiquitous conspiracy, having no other resource
left but his strong arm, he rolls up his sleeves and strikes,
blindly, rapturously, with an inordinate joy in the physical
performance. It is just such indulgence in violence which
the Jews felt was always ready to break loose from the inner
insecurity of this German type, and to which they are
particularly sensitive.

The Jews have fought well on battlefields in biblical as
well as in recent times. But, characteristically, physical
heroism has no prominent role in their tradition. Neither
the triumphs of Saul and David, nor the Herculian Samson
crushing the Philistines, nor the memorable rebellion of the
Maccabees have given rise to a Jewish heroic saga. The
Jews, an ancient people with many primitive traits, have no
heroic saga. In their chronicles, the subtler types always

prevail over the robust ones, Jacob over Esau, Joseph over his brothers, David over Goliath. And what the Bible essentially deals with are the deeds, not of giants and titans, but of the spiritual God.

During their long history the Jews have had such excessive opportunity to experience the stupidity and futility of violence that they are left with a profound disgust for it. And, more generally, what shocks them in the physical German is the transgression of the human form and dignity, the offense against man as the image of God, which inheres in every form of intoxication, in drunkenness, in a special inclination toward death as heroic self-assertion, in a tendency to merge in the rank and file, to be boundlessly absorbed by the function *per se,* the material *per se.* All this is utterly alien to the Jews; it is still, fundamentally and atavistically, the heathen whom they sense in it.

"German vices," says Nietzsche, "are their drunkenness and suicidal tendency (which are a proof of the clumsiness of their intellect)". And further: "Stiff awkwardness in intellectual attitudes and the clumsy fist in grasping—these things are German to such a degree as to be confounded abroad with the German character as a whole." And again: "They first of all wish to see their genuine craving for obedience idolized." And again: "Everyone who has to live among Germans suffers from . . . their formlessness, torpor and clumsiness. . . ." And so forth, and so on. But with all this Nietzsche actually does not characterize the German, he pictures the *goi.* In point of fact, for a precise and elaborate description of what the Jews mean by *goi,* we must refer to a German, Friedrich Nietzsche.

It has to be said, to be sure, that this human type can be found in *all* countries including America, more frequently in Northern than in Southern ones. But in Germany alone it has, for a time, come to dominate the country and the whole life of a people.

To summarize this inevitably all too sketchy presentation of the Judaeo-German problem: What I wanted to demonstrate is the fact that between Germans and Jews there existed a very special, unique relationship, an interpenetration of dispositions and destinies, which in both peoples, through accordances and discordances, touched the nerve of existence. Germany, never complete as a nation, remained a kind of open society, open to influences from everywhere, and so to the boundless eagerness of the Jews to find a homeland and to join in the universalistic tendency that had been alive for centuries in this special homeland. But the unfulfilled power aspirations, which persist in the physical and emotional depths of the Germans, reacted with the brutal force that has always been the last resort of the mentally helpless. So the physical Germans, getting the upper hand, wanted to rid the country, once and for all, of a relationship that had reached too deep. Just as the Christian Church wanted to cut itself off from an irksome, but indissoluble parentage by a lasting enslavement of the Jews, so the Nazis tried to extricate a Nordicized Germany from its all too close Jewish and Judaeo-Christian ties. And, body-minded as they were, they thought it could be done by killing off six million human beings.

In conclusion, an ultimate similarity between Germans and Jews may be mentioned. In both peoples the span is wide between their best and their worst. Of both peoples it may be said what the treatise Megilla in the Babylonian Talmud says of the Jews: "This people has been likened to the dust, it has been likened to the stars. Sinking, it is debased into dust. Rising, it is lifted to the stars."

APPENDIX

The Jews and the Arabs in Palestine:

A Disputation with Philip K. Hitti

ALBERT EINSTEIN and **ERICH KAHLER**

INTRODUCTORY NOTE

In February 1944, Dr. Philip K. Hitti, Professor of Semitic Literature at Princeton University, testified before the Committee on Foreign Affairs of the House of Representatives during the hearings on the Wright-Compton Resolution for the reconstitution of Palestine as a free and democratic Jewish commonwealth. The text of Dr. Hitti's testimony was published in the report of the hearings, issued by the Government Printing Office in 1944, under the title "The Jewish National Home." It was also featured in the *Princeton Herald* of April 7, 1944.

A reply to Professor Hitti's statement, jointly conceived by Dr. Albert Einstein and Dr. Erich Kahler, and written by Erich Kahler, appeared in the *Princeton Herald* of April 14, 1944. Professor Hitti's response to that statement appeared a week later, in the *Princeton Herald* of April 21. The controversy was concluded with Albert Einstein's and Erich Kahler's rejoinder of April 28, 1944.

Following is the text of the entire discussion as it appeared in the *Princeton Herald*, with the permission of Professor Hitti, who has kindly agreed to the republication of his statements as they relate to a controversy which is still going on.

Testimonial Statement by Philip K. Hitti

FROM THE Arab point of view, political Zionism is an exotic movement, internationally financed, artificially stimulated and holds no hope of ultimate or permanent success. Not only to the fifty million Arabs, many of whom are descendants of the Canaanites who were in the land long before the Hebrews entered Palestine under Joshua, but to the entire Moslem society, of whom the Arabs form the spearhead, a sovereign Jewish state in Palestine appears as an anachronism. These Moslems constitute a somewhat self-conscious society of about 275,000,000, who dominate a large portion of Africa and Asia. Even if the Zionist political program, supported by British and American diplomacy and bayonets, should some day become a reality, what chance of survival has such an alien state amidst a camp of a would-be hostile Arabic and unsympathetic Islamic

123

world? There was a time in which a foreign state, a Latin one, was established in the Holy Land, but its memory lives today only in books on the Crusades.

For, be it remembered, on no other issue did the Moslems in modern times seem to manifest such a unanimity. Even on the question of the restoration of the caliphate, after it was destroyed by Mustafa Kemal in 1924, there has been more friction and less solidarity, as evidenced by the proceedings of the Islamic congresses held in Cairo and Mecca. Verbal protests against the Zionist political program, which this resolution adopts, and cash to fight its provisions have poured in the last two decades from Morocco to Malay. In India a "Palestine Day" was celebrated in 1936 and the All Indian Moslem League passed a resolution at its annual session on October 18, 1939, and another in its April meeting of 1943, warning the British against converting Palestine into a Jewish state. Jerusalem in Moslem eyes is the third *haram*, the third holy city after Mecca and Medina. It was the first *giblah*, the first direction in which the early Moslems prayed before they began to turn in prayer toward Mecca. The land was given by Allah as a result of a *jihad* (holy war) and therefore for the Moslems to relinquish their claim on it constitutes a betrayal of their faith. It is even more sacred to the Christians, of whom there are some 130,000 in Palestine.

This uncompromising, persistent opposition to political Zionism, whose cause the resolution espoused, does not spell anti-Semitism. Of all the major peoples of the world, the Arabs perhaps come nearest to being free from race prejudice. Besides, they, like the Jews, are Semites, and they know it. They also know that their two religions are closest of kin, closer than either of them is to Christianity. Nowhere throughout medieval and modern times were Jews better treated than in Moslem-Arab lands. So welcome were American Jewish ambassadors to the Sublime Porte at Constantinople that our government appointed three of them in a row; Strauss, Elkus and Morgenthau.

These Arabs and Moslems cannot understand why the Jewish problem, which is not of their making, should be solved at their expense. They deeply sympathize with the afflicted Jews but are not convinced that Palestine solves the Jewish problem; Palestine does not qualify as a country without a people ready to receive a people without a country. They fail to understand why the American legislators, so solicitous for the welfare of the European Jews, should not lift the bars of immigration and admit Jewish refugees, millions of whom could be settled on the unoccupied plains of Arizona or Texas. This certainly falls within their jurisdiction. The word "reconstitute" in the resolution would no doubt interest them [the Arabs], and they would like to remake the map of Europe and put up their claim on Spain, which they held at a much later date and for a longer period of time. Some of them would raise the question how would the people of the United States react to a suggestion from, say, Russia, to reconstitute Oklahoma as an Indian territory. They realize they have no spokesmen in America, no high-pressure groups, no machinery for influencing American public opinion or legislation, but they are willing to rest their case upon its merits and upon America's sense of justice.

Some of them may have forgotten the Anglo-French declaration of November 8, 1918, promising the peoples so long oppressed by the Turks complete and definitive liberation and the establishment of national governments and administrations drawing their authority from the initiative and free choice of the indigenous population; or the words of Woodrow Wilson's twelfth point that the non-Turkish nationalities which are now under Turkish rule should be assured an undoubted security of life and an absolute opportunity of autonomous development; or the

corresponding provision in the Covenant of the League of
Nations, article 22; but they certainly do remember the
third article of the Atlantic Charter that Great Britain and
the United States respect the right of all peoples to choose
the form of government under which they will live.

*   *   *

No Westerner, or *Ifranji* as called in Arabic, is more highly
respected and more implicitly trusted by the Arab and
Moslem people than the American. There is reason for it.
For years American teachers, preachers, physicians, archae-
ologists, pilgrims and philanthropists have frequented the
eastern shore of the Mediterranean with the intent of
giving rather than taking and with no imperialistic de-
signs. The American press at Beirut, the first well-equipped
press in that region, celebrated its hundredth anniversary
eight years ago. The American University of Beirut celebrated its seventy-fifth anniversary three years ago. In this
institution a large part of the leaders of thought and action
throughout the Arab East were trained. In the First World
War and the immediate period following, no less than one
hundred million dollars were raised by the American public to relieve suffering among the people of the Near East
and to rehabilitate their land—an unparalleled figure in the
history of private philanthropy. No wonder the word
"American " has become associated in the minds of Arabs
and Moslems with fair play, honorable dealing and democratic conduct. All their reservoir of goodwill accumulated
through generations of unselfish and hard-working Americans will be threatened with destruction by the passage of
the resolution now before this committee.

The United States is now engaged in a life-and-death
struggle with an unscrupulous, powerful, and far-from-
being-beaten enemy. No drier and more explosive powder
could we provide for his propaganda weapons. The Ger-

mans, we can be sure, will fully capitalize this resolution—
as they did the Balfour declaration, hold it out before Arab
eyes as a sample of the kind of Anglo-American democracy
and freedom for which this war is fought, and assure the
Arabs that the Zionist control of Palestine is but the prelude
to the Jewish control of Trans-Jordan, Syria, Lebanon,
Arabia—the camel's head intruding into the tent about
which they read in their *Arabian Nights*. This is no time
to turn old friends into potential enemies.

The people of the United States are not only interested
in winning the war, but in contributing to the establishment of a postwar world order in which regional stability
is somewhat secure and the chances of future conflicts are
at least reduced. Nothing, in the judgment of the speaker,
is more conducive to a state of perpetual unrest and conflict
than the establishment of a Jewish commonwealth at the
expense of the Arabs in Palestine. If such a commonwealth
were established at the insistence of the United States, we
then assume moral responsibility for its preservation. Will
the people of the United States be willing to send their
navy to protect such a commonwealth if established?

The British never contemplated such an ambitious
scheme as the conversion of Palestine into a Jewish commonwealth. Sandwiched between conflicting promises to
the Arabs (which made the once-promised land multi-
promised), the Balfour Declaration, which was echoed in
the United States Congress resolution of 1922, viewed with
favor the establishment in Palestine of a national home for
the Jewish people—a quite different thing from converting Palestine into a Jewish state. And that was viewed
with a big proviso: It being understood that nothing shall
be done which may prejudice the civil and religious rights
of non-Jewish communities in Palestine. The Zionist representatives proposed to the then British government this
text, "The reconstitution of Palestine as the national home
of the Jewish people," which is practically the same as the

resolution before us has it; but that was not the text adopted.

In its White Paper of June 3, 1922, the British government stated:

"Unauthorized statements have been made to the effect that the purpose in view is to create a wholly Jewish Palestine. Phrases have been used such as that Palestine is to become as Jewish as England is English. His Majesty's Government regard such expectation as unpracticable and have no such aim in view. They would draw attention to the fact that the terms of the Declaration referred to do not contemplate that Palestine as a whole be converted into a Jewish national home but that such a home should be founded in Palestine. When it is asked what is meant by the development of a Jewish national home in Palestine, it may be answered that it is not the imposition of a Jewish nationality upon the inhabitants of Palestine as a whole, but the further development of the existing Jewish community, with the assistance of Jews from other parts of the world, in order that it may become a center in which the Jewish people as a whole may take, on grounds of religion and race, an interest and a pride."

In its statement of Policy of 1937 the British government declared: "That their obligations to Arabs and Jews respectively were not incompatible, on the assumption that in the process of time the two races would so adjust their national aspirations as to render possible the establishment of a single commonwealth under a unitary government."

In the 1939 statement it was again made clear that Palestine shall be constituted a sovereign independent state, a Palestinian state in which all Palestinians—irrespective of race or origin—will be citizens enjoying equal political, civil, and religious rights. In that statement the provision was made for limiting Jewish immigration for economic as well as political reasons. Even then the British administration of Palestine has been confronted throughout its history with a series of strikes and disturbances, beginning April 1920, and culminating in the serious revolution of 1936.

As early as August 1919, and before Arab nationalism attained the intensity that it has since assumed, the King-Crane Commission sent by President Wilson reported as follows: "A national home for the Jewish people is not equivalent to making Palestine into a Jewish State; nor can the erection of such a Jewish State be accomplished without the greatest trespass upon the civil and religious rights of existing non-Jewish communities in Palestine." The report warned that the Zionist program could not be carried out except by force of arms. "The more enlightened and realistic among the Zionists themselves have begun to . . . concentrate on the cultural and spiritual aspects of their cause and cooperate with the Arabs."

Dr. John L. Magnes, President of the Hebrew University of Jerusalem—a Zionist institution—declared in September 1941: "As far as I am able to see, there is no chance whatsoever that this formula, establishment of Palestine as a Jewish commonwealth instead of a national home in Palestine, would be acceptable by any responsible Arab or Arab party or any part of Arabic public opinion." The Union Association, organized in September 1942 by Zionists in Jerusalem, declared its conviction that the problem of Palestine was inseparable from that of the Near East, advocated a Jewish Arab state and held that the two peoples' equality was vital to the future of Palestine. Robert M. Hyanson, British Zionist, in *Palestine: A Policy* (1942), interprets national as pertaining to nationality rather than nation. President Julian Morganstern, of Hebrew Union College, Cincinnati, in his latest contribution entitled *Nation, People, Religion: What Are We?* declares

Despite the oft-repeated, high sounding assertions of the beneficent role which a restored Jewish state or commonwealth may play or will play in setting a happy pattern of equitable social relations for all other nations to emulate, the most recent formulation of which is in the highly bombastic peroration of the so-called Palestine resolution of the American Jewish Conference, the fact incontestably established by history still confronts us with brazen truth, that the true genius and destiny of Israel find expression only in its role as a religious people, the bearers of a spiritual heritage."

Thus we see that the passage of this resolution now before your Committee is inimical to the best interests of the Arabs, the Americans, the British, and even the Jews.

Answer: by Albert Einstein and Erich Kahler

THE PRESENTATION of the Palestine problem by Professor Hitti is so one-sided that it cannot go unanswered. Before considering Professor Hitti's views we want, however, to state that we do not speak in the name of the Zionist movement but as non-partisan Jews and plain human beings.

Professor Hitti defends the Arab stand on ethical, religious, and political grounds. The Arabs, he says, are descendants of the ancient Canaanites who held the land before the Jews. Jerusalem is to the Arabs the third holy city, it is the direction in which the early Arabs prayed, and the land was given to them by Allah as the result of a *jihad,* a holy war.

We do not believe that in our epoch these are the real issues that influence the turn of events, but we have to deal with them as stressed by Professor Hitti.

Both Jews and Arabs are said to stem from a common ancestor, from Abraham, who immigrated into Canaan (i.e., Palestine), and so neither of them seem to have been earlier in the land than the other. Recent views assume that only part of the Israelites migrated to Egypt—as reflected in the Joseph story—and part of them remained in Palestine. So part of the Canaanite population encountered by the Jews when they entered the Promised Land under Joshua were Israelites, too. Therefore, the Arabs have no priority on the land.

To the Arabs Jerusalem is only the third holy city, to the Jews it is the first and only holy city, and Palestine is the place where their original history, their sacred history took place. Besides, to the Arabs Jerusalem is a holy city only insofar as they trace their tradition back to Jewish origins, insofar as after the Arab conquest of Jerusalem in 637, the "Omar Mosque," the "Dome of the Rock" was erected by the Omayyad Caliph Abd el Malek on the very place where the Jewish Ark of the Covenant and the Temple of Solomon had stood, on a rock *even shetijah* (world foundation stone), which was considered by the Jews as reaching down to the bottom of the cosmic ocean, the navel of the world. And Jerusalem was a *gibah*, a direction of prayer, under Mohammed only as long as he counted on the Jews as the main supporters of his new creed; he changed it, when his hopes failed, together with other institutions established out of pure consideration for his Jewish adherents, as for instance fasting on the Jewish Day of Atonement. The first *gibah* has, therefore, as much validity for the Arabs as the Jewish Day of Atonement—both are today abolished in their religious significance. It seems a little far-fetched to use this abrogated rite as evidence on which to base the Arab claim to Palestine.

If, finally, the Arab conquest of Palestine is considered holy, it would be only fair to admit the corresponding holiness of the peaceful claim and the peaceful reclamation of the country by the Jews. To refer to the legitimacy of a "holy war" sounds rather queer for a people which denounces peaceful immigration as a violation of their rights. No wonder Professor Hitti, on the one hand, uses the overwhelming Arab power as a threat and, on the other, plays on the Nazi insinuations to which the Arab world is said to be highly susceptible; that a tiny Jewish community in Palestine of two or three million at the most would become a danger to four mighty Arab states and fifty million Arabs.

But the Jews do not resort to arguments of power or of priority. One does not get very far with historical rights. Very few peoples of the world would be entitled to their present countries if such a criterion were applied. Professor Hitti says the Arabs cannot understand why the Jewish problem which is not of their making should be solved at their expense. But by their holy war and their conquest of Palestine the Arabs contributed their share to depriving the Jews of their homeland and so to the making of the Jewish problem, even though one must concede that their share is comparatively smaller than that of other peoples. The stand the Arabs take, however, with regard to the Jews, is exactly the one which all peoples of the world are taking. No people, unfortunately, understands why it should contribute anything to the solution of the Jewish problem. The surface of the globe is everywhere occupied, and wherever the Jews could be given a piece of land under fair climatic conditions they would encroach on some property rights and sovereignties and would face friction with a population already firmly established on the spot. No country has been found where the Jews could possibly form an autonomous community, however small.

There is still one difference between other peoples and the Arabs. Every people has one country of its own which it developed with all the care of generations, and none of these countries has any connection with a specifically Jewish tradi-

tion or concern. The Arabs possess seven major countries—
Saudi Arabia, which harbors their holy places, Yemen,
Egypt, Iraq, Syria, Transjordania, Lebanon, if we leave aside
the North African colonies and provinces as yet not en-
franchised from European rule. And the least and obviously
most neglected of their settlements was the part they occupied in the tiny Palestinian country; only nine hundred
thousand of fifty million Arabs live there. This tiny Palestinian country, on the other hand, is the only place in the
world legitimately and most deeply connected with the Jewish people, its religious foundation, and its historic tradition
as an independent people.

In order to clarify the Palestinian problem let us compare the situation of the Jews with that of the Arabs. The
Jews are and have always been numerically a small people.
They have never exceeded fifteen and a half million. De-
prived of their homeland through the ancient and medieval
conquests of Palestine they lived dispersed all over the
world, and what they have suffered since by persecutions,
expulsions and tortures of all kinds is far beyond anything
the other peoples had to endure. Of the fifteen and a half
million computed in 1938 at least two million* have been
slaughtered or starved to death by the Nazis in the various
European countries during the past few years. So the
Zionist movement, or better the striving for a haven in the
place of Jewish origin, is by no means an "exotic, artificially
stimulated movement" as Professor Hitti calls it, but a
movement urged forward by utter need and distress.

The promise held out to the Jews in the Balfour Declaration after the First World War has been whittled down
bit by bit in the course of the British appeasement policy,
yielding to interests partly British, partly Arabian—a policy
bitterly denounced by Churchill himself before he became
Prime Minister. Palestine is a link in the lifeline of the

* Since the appearance of this article, the figure has been officially
computed as six millions.

British Empire between the Near East and India; and the Jewish people, by necessity a dependable ally of the British, have been sacrificed to the Arabs who, by their numerical and political strength and the trump of the Islamic portion of the Indian population, were in a position to sell even their neutrality dearly in the present conflict. The final result has been the complete prohibition* of Jewish immigration into Palestine at the very moment when more hundreds of thousands of Jews were threatened with annihilation by the Hitler armies occupying Hungary and Rumania.

We invite every fair-minded American to look at the photos in a recent account of the martyrdom of Polish Jewry under Nazi occupation, published by the American Federation of Polish Jews (*The Black Book of Polish Jewry*, 1943), and to read the report of an American and non-Jewish eye-witness, Walter Clay Lowdermilk, an expert in land cultivation who traveled through the Near East to study the land record of that region (*Palestine, Land of Promise*, 1944).

"During my stay in Palestine in 1939 [Dr. Lowdermilk tells us], I witnessed a tragic by-product of the German advance into Czechoslovakia. In Palestine and Syria we were told of old cargo boats, filled with refugees from Nazi-dominated Central Europe . . . whose miserable passengers were not permitted to land anywhere because of the lack of formal visas. We saw those wretched ships floating about on a steaming sea in unbearable summer heat with refugees packed in holds under intolerably inhuman conditions. The laws governing the transportation of animals for slaughter

---

* By the terms of the Palestine White Paper of 1939, no new immigration certificates for Palestine have been issued since April 1, 1944. Only a few thousand certificates now remain from the 75,000 quota set by the White Paper [as of late 1944—E.K.].

in the United States do not permit conditions like those which some of the intelligentsia of Central Europe had to undergo in these old boats on the Mediterranean. The revolting slave ships of a century ago were better; for slaves had a slave value and their ships were sped to their destination without delay. But Jewish refugees were kept floating about upon a torrid sea, just out of sight, with the desperate hope that the captain . . . would attempt to discharge them illegally on the shores of Palestine.

"During our stay in Beirut, an old cargo boat, loaded with 655 refugees . . . was unloaded at the quarantine station for a few days. The ship was so overrun with rats that the passengers had to be removed to exterminate this vermin. We found that they had been floating about for eleven weeks, packed into little wooden shells built around the four cargo holds. The congestion, the ghastly unsanitary conditions and sufferings that these people had undergone aroused our highest admiration for their courage and fortitude. We were astonished to find that these former citizens of Czechoslovakia represented a very high level of European culture . . . 42 were lawyers, 40 were engineers, 26 were physicians and surgeons, in addition to women doctors, professional writers, gifted musicians, pharmacists and nurses. . . . Without passports, without country, these useful and highly cultured refugees presented one of the most tragic spectacles of modern times. No ambassador, no consul spoke up for them to demand the rights and privileges enjoyed by the lowliest citizen of the smallest country."

This is the Jewish situation; and there is no guarantee whatever against the persistence or recurrence of anti-Semitic outbreaks everywhere after this war. Even if we put aside the spiritual, religious and cultural ties making Palestine the

only place in the world which persecuted Jews could consider as their home and develop with all the devotion a
homeland inspires—there is no other country in the world
acceptable to human beings which the numerous refugee
conferences were able to offer to this hounded people. The
Jews are prepared for extreme sacrifices and the hardest
work to convert this narrow strip which is Palestine into a
prosperous country and model civilization.

What Jewish youth has already achieved in the few decades of Zionist settlement may be gathered from Dr. Lowdermilk's book. They took over from the period of Arabian
predominance deserts and rocks and barren soil and turned
them into flowering farms and plantations, into forests and
modern cities. They created new forms of cooperative settlements and raised the living standards of the Arabian
and the Jewish population alike. The Jews are willing and
ready to give any guarantee of protection for the holy
places and the civil rights, indeed the autonomy, of Arabs
and Christians, a guarantee safeguarded by the overwhelming power of their neighbors on whose cooperation they
depend. They offer their assistance and their experience
for the economic and scientific advancement of the Arab
countries, for the lifting of their population to a modern
standard of living.

But this, unfortunately, is just what the Arab leaders do
not want. For the true source of Arab resistance and hostility toward a Jewish Palestine is neither religious nor political, but social and economic. The Arabian population of
Palestine is negligible in comparison with the vast number of Arab elements in the European provinces of North
Africa and Asia. The Arabian chieftains did not arouse the
Moslem world against Mussolini's regime in Libya; most
of them were on splendid terms with him. The Mufti of
Jerusalem and other Arab leaders were greatly honored
guests in Rome. The rich Arabian landowners did nothing
to improve the nature, the civilization, or the living stan-

dards of their countries. The large Arabian states are underpopulated, the masses of the people are held in a
backward and inferior condition. "Life in the Damascus
of the eighth century was not greatly different from what
it is today," says Professor Hitti in his book about the Arabs
[*History of the Arabs*, 1937]. But the big Effendis fear the
example and the impulse which the Jewish colonization of
Palestine presents to the peoples of the Near East, they
resent the social and economic uplift of the Arabian workers in Palestine. They act as all fascist forces have acted:
they screen their fear of social reform behind nationalistic
slogans and demagoguery. If it were not for these leaders
and instigators, perfect agreement and cooperation could
be achieved between the Arab and the Jewish people.

The purpose of this statement is not a nationalistic one.
We do not, and the vast majority of the Jews do not, ad-
vocate the establishment of a state for the sake of national
greed and self-glorification, which would run counter to all
the traditional values of Judaism and which we consider
obsolete everywhere. In speaking up for a Jewish Palestine,
we want to promote the establishment of a place of refuge
where persecuted human beings may find security and
peace and the undisputed right to live under a law and
order of their making. The experiences of many centuries
have taught us that this can be provided only by home
rule and not by a foreign administration. This is why we
stand for a Jewish-controlled Palestine, be it ever so mod-
est and small. We do not refer to historic rights, although
if there is anything like a historic right to a country, the
Jews can claim it in Palestine, at least as well as the Arabs.
We do not resort to threats of power, for the Jews have
no power; they are, in fact, the most powerless group on
earth. If they had had any power they should have been
able to prevent the annihilation of millions of their people
and the closing of the last door to the helpless victims of
the Nazis. What we appeal to is an elementary sense of

justice and humanity. We know how weak such a position is, but we also know that if the arguments of threats of power, of sacred egoisms and holy wars continue to prevail in the future world order, not only the Jews but the whole of humanity will be doomed.

Reply: by Philip K. Hitti

DR. EINSTEIN and Dr. Kahler introduce their criticism of my testimony before the House Committee on Foreign Relations by describing it as "one-sided." After several days of favorable Zionist testimony, I was called upon, in accordance with longstanding democratic practice, to present the other side. And my testimony was followed by that of many other Zionists and proved to be, with one exception, the only one which presented the other side.

The first issue that the two distinguished writers take with me is a historical one. They maintain that "the Arabs have no priority on the land," because "Both Jews and Arabs are said to stem from a common ancestor, from Abraham, who immigrated into Canaan (i.e., Palestine)." But when Abraham—assuming his historicity—migrated into Canaan he did not find it empty, as even a superficial acquaintance with the Old Testament literature would indicate. The so-called Arabs of Palestine, particularly the Christians among them, are the modern representatives of that ancient native stock. The Hebrews came and went. The natives remained. The Hebrew Kingdom of Israel was destroyed in 722 B.C. by the Assyrian Sargon II; that of Judah by Nebuchadnezzar in 586 B.C. First the ten, then the two tribes were carried away into captivity. All flickers of national life were extinguished by later rulers and the hold of the Jews over Palestine was gone forever.

The two authors then proceeded to dispute another historical point. They claim that the Moslem "Arabs contributed their share to depriving the Jews of their homeland and so to the making of the Jewish problem." The two critics evidently are not aware of the fact that the Moslems conquered Palestine in the seventh century after Christ (Palestine was then Christian not Jewish) from the Byzantines, who were the heirs of the Romans, who had wrested it from the Seleucids, who were successors of Alexander the Great, who had acquired it from the Persians, who had destroyed the Chaldaean Empire in 538 B.C., which had controlled Palestine since Nebuchadnezzar's conquest. A casual acquaintance with *History of the Arabs*, which the two gentlemen quote in another connection, would have spared them this error. But obviously Dr. Einstein's acquaintance with the antecedents and setting of the Arab-Zionist problem does not far surpass my acquaintance with his theory of relativity.

Using my testimony as a springboard, the two scholars ignore the arguments presented against political Zionism from the British, the American and Jewish points of view and proceed to present the orthodox Zionist doctrine, claiming at the same time that they "do not speak in the name of the Zionist movement." The arguments they give are a rehash of the Zionist arguments repeated over years, and intensified in recent months, from the radio, platform, newspapers, books, and propaganda sheets. None of the arguments hold water when subjected to close scrutiny.

The first may be termed the argument of the "have-nots" against the "haves." "The Arabs possess seven major countries," we are told. "This tiny Palestinian country, on the other hand, is the only place in the world legitimately and most deeply connected with the Jewish people." Does not this strike a familiar note to the readers of apologies for modern aggression? Immigration and colonization, be it remembered, are a form of attenuated invasion. In the case of political Zionism, they are a professed though peaceful invasion implied in the resolution before the Congressional committees in Washington:

"That the United States shall use its good offices and take appropriate measures to the end that the doors of Palestine shall be opened for free entry into that country, and that there shall be full opportunity for colonization so that the Jewish people may ultimately reconstitute Palestine as a free and democratic Jewish commonwealth."

In one of the official British Commission's reports, the process of Jewish penetration is termed by the Arabs a "creeping conquest," and a creeping conquest it is. In a recent note of protest to Washington from Iraq, the passage of this resolution was declared as tantamount to a declaration of war by the United States on the Arabs of Palestine.

From the above often-repeated argument, Dr. Einstein and his collaborator proceeded to another often-repeated argument: the humanitarian one, emphasizing the plight of European Jews under Hitler's heel and the necessity for alleviating their misery. What makes the position of those opposing the "reconstituting of Palestine as a Jewish commonwealth" (and all organized opposition in the United States comes from the Jews themselves) rather embarrassing is that they may seem irresponsive to the humane call. The fact is that in the discussion that followed the testimony in Washington the present writer declared as an American citizen that he would welcome legislation admitting Jews and non-Jews to these shores. The official attitude of our government toward the refugee problem was expressed by Assistant Secretary Breckenridge Long in recent testimony before a Congressional committee where, after discussing the recommendations of the Bermuda Conference headed by our own President Dodds, Mr. Long made it clear that the Jewish refugee problem could not be isolated and that the government could not exclude persons other than Jews from its activities.

What makes the action of the scores of Amercian senators, representatives, governors (Dewey included) and other high officials who in this year of election have seen fit to sign the numerous Zionist manifestos appear hypocritical is the fact that none of these gentlemen seem willing to raise a finger to lift the bars of immigration into the United States. Let the British force the Palestinians, who have already witnessed the advent of hundreds of thousands of Jews into their midst in the last twenty years, to admit more Zionists until they become a majority and rule the land. Such in short is their easy solution of one of the world's knottiest problems!

The third argument, also a familiar one, advanced by Einstein and Kahler, is what may be termed the successful cultivation of the soil. "They [the Zionists] took over from the period of Arabian predominance deserts and rocks and barren soil and turned them into flowering farms and plantations, into forests and modern cities." This also has a customary ring in the ears of those who listened to—for example—Italian apologists in Tripoli (1912) and in Ethiopia (1935). But be that as it may; anyone with first-hand knowledge of the real economic situation can prick this bubble of highly publicized, greatly advertised "Palestinian prosperity." The plain truth is that the Zionist colonies are still living on charity. The difference between their prosperity and the genuine thing is precisely the difference between a plump healthy cheek with red blood corpuscles and a puffed-up one smeared with rouge. The Palestine Homeland is at present forty percent self-supporting, according to British estimates. The American Consul General in Jerusalem reports that $5,500,000 are poured annually from the United States alone to support it. Let this process of "artificial respiration" cease and it would not be difficult to see what would happen. The unbalanced condition of the whole country's economy may be evidenced by the fact that from 1926 to 1927 imports exceeded exports by as much as 5–1, and from 1937 to 1939 by 2½–1. As for the advantages which we have been repeatedly told have accrued to the native population, suffice it to quote article 3 of the constitution of the enlarged Jewish Agency signed at Zurich, August 14, 1929: "The land acquired shall be held as the inalienable property of the Jewish people," (a provision to this effect is incorporated in every lease), and "in all the works or undertakings carried out or furthered by the Agency it shall be deemed to be a matter of principle that Jewish labor shall be employed"—a perpetual boycott against Arab labor.

The statement of Dr. Einstein and Dr. Kahler ends on a meek note. "We do not resort to threats of power, for the Jews have no power," etc., which does not exactly jibe with recent declarations of Zionist spokesmen and with the reports about smuggling of arms, and the manufacture of hand grenades and explosion of bombs in the Zionist parts of Palestine. Ziff, a Zionist spokesman, would "make the Arabs go back to the desert where they came from." Weizmann, the head of Zionism, would "facilitate" Arab transference from Palestine. Ben Horin is more frank. He, as announced in his book and full-page advertisements in the *New York Times*, endorsed by scores of prominent and wealthy Americans, would solve the problem once and for all by transferring the Arab population not only of Palestine but of Trans-Jordan also into Iraq to make room for Zionists. Militant Zionism is a quite different thing from what my two distinguished neighbors seem to take it to be.

Sober and realistic Jews realize that it is on such stuff as presented by militant and political Zionism that anti-Semitism feeds. They recognize the unpracticability of the Zionist political program, consider Judaism a religion and not a political state, and admit that the great contribution of Israel throughout the ages has been in the spiritual and intellectual rather than the political realm. They have no desire to deprive the Arab population of its civil rights, guaranteed in the Balfour Declaration, and would like to see a *Palestinian* state—neither Jewish nor Moslem—in which all citizens, regardless of faith or origin become equal and free citizens. They know for a fact that when the present war is over many of the European Jews would want to return to their old homelands of which they were citizens first and Jews second; unless this war makes it safe for European Jews and non-Jews to live in harmony and peace it would have been fought in vain. As American Jewish citizens, they must have received the latest reports that of the five thousand five hundred American Jews now in Palestine only one hundred have forsaken their American citizenship and the rest are worried to death lest this war be so prolonged that they would lose their opportunity to return to the States, at least to renew their passports. The sober and realistic Arabs are likewise beginning to realize that many of the Jews now in Palestine are there to stay, and that the Arabs' own interest and future welfare require that they cooperate with these newcomers on an equal basis to the end that a new Palestine shall arise worthy of its honored name and noble heritage.

Conclusion: by Albert Einstein and Erich Kahler

PROFESSOR HITTI found some minor "bubbles" of ours to prick while leaving the major ones undisturbed. As we shall presently see, however, even those he pricked still float in the sun.

There is first the annoying question of priority. The

Arabs of Palestine, who are now introduced as "so-called Arabs," are said to stem from the population settled in the land before the immigration of Abraham whom the religious tradition of the Arabs considers their ancestor. This would separate the Palestinian Arabs racially from the rest of the Arabian people. But if Professor Hitti has his originally Canaanite Amurru, or Amorites, from whom to derive the Palestinian Arabs, we have our Chitti, or Hittites, who also belong to the early Canaanite population and to whom some scholars, and Professor Hitti among them, partly trace back the Jews. And so we would be on the same point of parity again. Yet all these racial genealogies can neither be proved nor disproved, they are entirely hypothetical, and highly precarious at that. Many populations were swept into the country during the stormy millennia of the early period, many migrations, multifold intermingling occurred, as indicated in the biblical stories, so that the relation of the present "so-called Arabs" to the early Canaanites can hardly be considered "descent." Besides, as we have pointed out before, this whole issue of priority counts for nothing in the actual apportionment of our globe and in the presence of our most urgent contemporary problems.

As to the question of the Arab conquest of Palestine, we too have heard of Nebuchadnezzar and Cyrus and Alexander the Great and Titus, and we referred to their conquests in our article. We were even aware of the fact that the Moslems wrested Palestine from the Byzantine Christians, and not from the Jews. But the Arabian conquest of Palestine, having been proclaimed as a holy war, established the Arab claim to the control of the country and even in the twentieth century induced an Arab scholar, Professor Hitti, to state that "The land was given by Allah as a result of a *jihad* (holy war) and therefore for the Moslems to relinquish their claim on it constitutes a betrayal of their faith." In this way the Arab conquest of

Palestine had indeed contributed its share of depriving the Jews of their homeland.

Professor Hitti says: "The Hebrews came and went. The natives remained." Now the fact is that the Israelites—we prefer to use this term because the Arabs also belong to the "Hebrew" peoples—the Israelites came, but they never went. From Professor Hitti's picture one would gain the impression that Jewish history in Palestine did not amount to very much after the destruction of the kingdoms of Israel and Judah and the Babylonian captivity in the sixth century B.C. A few "flickers of national life," that's all. But after the Babylonian captivity the second great period, a true renaissance, of Jewish Palestine began, leading, on the one hand, to the elaboration of the Palestinian Talmud and, on the other, to the birth of Christianity from Judaism. If we were vindictive we could ask Professor Hitti whether he knows something of the revolt of the Maccabees and the ensuing independent Kingdom of the Hasmoneans lasting nearly a century. He knows, of course.

It was as late as A.D. 429 that the Jewish Patriarchate in Palestine was abolished. Jewish communities persisted in Palestine uninterruptedly throughout the ages. In the tenth century the Arab writer, Mukadassi, complained about the predominance of the Jewish population in Jerusalem. From the fifteenth century on, the city of Safed in Upper Galilee became a flowering Jewish intellectual center where the mystical philosophy of the Kabbalah was taught and perfected. It lasted until it was wiped out by the Turkish governor in the seventeenth century. Spanish Jews, after their expulsion, sought refuge in their homeland of old; messianic movements in the eighth, seventeenth, and eighteenth centuries aimed at the liberation and reestablishment of Jewish Palestine. And constantly from all over the world Jewish individuals who felt their end approaching made pilgrimages to the Holy Land to die and be buried in its sacred soil.

Professor Hitti terms Jewish immigration into Palestine an "attenuated invasion" and a "creeping conquest." The difference between a regular conquest and this "creeping conquest" is that the one results in the ruin, the other in the rise of the "conquered" population. The improvement of the living conditions of the Arabs through the Zionist enterprise is an established fact confirmed by British official reports. The British Royal Commission that investigated Palestine in the winter of 1936-37 made the following statements:

"(1) The large import of Jewish capital into Palestine had a fructifying effect on the economic life of the country. (2) The expansion of Arab industry and citriculture has been largely financed by the capital thus obtained. (3) Jewish example has done much to improve Arab cultivation, especially citrus. (4) Owing to Jewish development and enterprise the employment of Arab labor has increased in urban areas, particularly in the ports. (5) The reclamation and anti-malaria work undertaken in Jewish villages have benefited all Arabs in the neighbourhood. (6) Institutions founded with Jewish funds primarily to serve the National Home, have also served the Arab population. Hadassah, for example, notably at the Tuberculosis Institute at Jerusalem, admits Arab country folk to the clinics of the Rural Sick Benefit Fund and does much infant welfare work for Arab mothers. (7) The general beneficent effect of Jewish immigration on Arab welfare is illustrated by the fact that the increase in the Arab population is most marked in urban areas affected by Jewish development. (8) The whole range of public services has steadily developed to the benefit of the fellaheen (the Arab peasants) . . . the revenue available for those services having been largely provided by the Jews."

The Jewish Agency, being intended for the promotion of Jewish enterprise, is, of course, bound to patronize Jewish labor. This is far from signifying a boycott against the Arabs. Arab workers are employed in great numbers in privately owned Jewish plantations and industries. Wages in Palestine are more than double those in Syria and three times as high as those in Iraq.

Let us compare general conditions in Palestine with those in Arab-ruled countries. "The situation of the fellaheen in Iraq is very poor," says W. C. Lowdermilk, "in fact, even in overpopulated China I never saw conditions so bad as those I found in the underpopulated but potentially rich lands of the Tigris-Euphrates Valley." Another expert on the country, Ernest Main, reports: "The fellaheen and coolie classes were living on less than a penny a day per head. . . . There are probably about two million people in the country living on such standards, and it can be imagined what purchasing power they possess, and what revenue they can offer."

As to the conditions of the peasants in Trans-Jordan which is included in the British Mandate for Palestine, the High Commissioner, Sir Arthur Wauchope, pointed out at the Twenty-seventh Session of the Permanent Mandates Commission: "Owing to the tax-payer's poverty [the Government] could only be carried on by means of grants-in-aid"—by charity Professor Hitti would say. It was only because Arab peasants and workers found better living conditions in Palestine, that between 1933 and 1936, for instance, more than thirty thousand Arabs from Iraq, Syria, Trans-Jordan and even the Arabian desert migrated to Palestine. There was twice as much Arab emigration from the Arab countries as from Palestine.

To reproach Palestinian economy with not being self-supporting, as Professor Hitti does, is equivalent to blaming a child for being dependent on its family. Jewish economy had to be built up from scratch, land had to be purchased at prices far higher than the land was actually worth, three or four times as high as a similar type of land would sell for in Syria or in Southern California. Machinery, fertilizer, and raw materials were lacking. And still, even Professor Hitti has to admit that imports decreased by fifty percent from 1927 to 1937. On the prospects of the country we may refer to the testimony of Sir Charles Warren, one of the British scholars of the Palestine Exploration Fund, who wrote as early as 1875: "Give Palestine a good government and increase the commercial life of the people and they may increase tenfold and yet there is room." And no suspicion of bias can certainly arise as to the statement of T. E. Lawrence, "Lawrence of Arabia," one of the most ardent friends the Arabs ever had: "Palestine was a decent country [in ancient times], and could so easily be made so again. The sooner the Jews farm it all the better: their colonies are bright spots in a desert."

There is one point on which we may agree with Professor Hitti: the Jews too have their diehards and their terrorists—although proportionally far less than other peoples. We do not shield or excuse these extremists. They are a product of the bitter experience that in our present world only threats and violence are rewarded and that fairness, sincerity and consideration get the worst of it. As far as Dr. Weizmann is concerned, however, we have to correct Professor Hitti's quotation. He never threatened the Arabs with expulsion. The passage to which Professor Hitti refers reads:

"There will be complete civil and political equality of rights for all citizens without distinction of race or religion, and, in addition, the Arabs will enjoy full autonomy in their own internal affairs. But if any Arabs do not wish to remain in a Jewish state, every facility will be given to them to transfer to one of the many and vast Arab countries."

There was a time, in 1919, when a perfect Arab-Jewish-British agreement was worked out by the late King Feisal—a nobler brand of leader than the present chiefs—Dr. Weizmann and T. E. Lawrence. Feisal declared:

". . . the Arabs, especially the educated among us, look with deepest sympathy on the Zionist movement . . . . Interested parties have been enabled to make capital out of what they call our differences . . . . I wish to give you my firm conviction that these differences . . . are easily dispelled by mutual good will."

Let us close our discussion with the fervent hope that this spirit of the great Arab leader will dominate the postwar arrangements and that matters will be decided not on the narrow scope of vested interests and local prevalences but from the broad point of view of human welfare at large.

ERICH KAHLER is internationally known for his distinguished contributions to the philosophy of history, *Man the Measure: A New Approach to History; The Tower and the Abyss: An Inquiry into the Transformation of Man;* and *The Meaning of History.* For eight years Professor of German and Comparative Literature at Cornell University, Dr. Kahler was also on the faculty of Princeton and Ohio State Universities. A former member of the Institute for Advanced Studies, Princeton, he is a fellow of the Leo Baeck Institute, where he has lectured on Jewish history and where two of these essays were first presented.

DATE